Custom-Fit

YOUR

Golf Swing

Go Beyond Swing Methods and
Find Your Best Swing with
The I-Swing System™

Dori O'Rourke

Published by:

www.NexStepGolf.com
(800) 743-4-FUN

First Printing: July 2006

Lead Editors: Tom "Chico" Chicovsky and
               Marion Caldwell
Illustrations: Bill Frederick
Cover Design: Ryan Belong
Back Cover Photo: Phyllis Furumoto
Male Photo Model: Sean O'Rourke
Female Photo Model: Janelle Lunsford
Cameo Appearance: Jeremy Lunsford

ISBN 978-0-9628854-3-3

Printed in the United States of America

3 5 7 9 10 8 6 4 2

THANK YOU!

My Family

Grandpa Bud
Mom and Lee
Bonnie and Budman
Sean and Christel
Brian, Christopher and Toireasa-Marie
Bret and Patty
Brandon, Riley and Tanner
Brian and Family
Aunt Dee and Uncle B

My Friends and Supporters

Janelle and Jeremy
Roger and Anne
Ed and Linda
Rick and Joyce
Roger and Nance
Walt and Donna

Kris and Carole
Ed and Barbara
Dick and Carol
Susan and Dana
Al and Marilyn

My Editing Team and Friends

The Dynamic Duo – Chico and Marion; Coach Bates, Linda, Larry, Collene, Norm from New York, Dennis, Bob C., Bob F., Bob D., Tom E., Cindy, Nancy, Yuri, and Rocky

My Teachers and Students

Whether on the golf course or in the course of life, I've learned so much from you!

Contents

The Front 9

⭐ The Back 9 ⭐

The 19ᵗʰ Hole

Introduction

Swing Methods Have Been the Norm

I've had the great pleasure of meeting hundreds of teaching professionals through the years, LPGA certified, PGA certified, and others. I've also watched many of them teach golf lessons. In almost every case, what touches me most is how deeply golf instructors care about their students.

They teach because they want their students to succeed. That is one of their greatest satisfactions and they are committed to doing whatever they can to help their students get the results they want.

The next thing that strikes me about most golf professionals is their passion for the golf swing. After years of studying the swing, both as players and instructors, most have a very strong belief about which swing method is best.

In fact, swing beliefs are often held so strongly that a debate over differing methods can sometimes match the intensity of a heated political or religious discussion!

Which Swing Method Do You Believe In?

Whether you're a teaching professional, playing professional, or amateur golfer, you probably have a swing method you believe in, too. For the first 15 years of my teaching career, I know I did. My swing beliefs changed over time, but I always had one way of swinging that I thought was best.

For me though, it wasn't about the method, it was about the results. I never taught a swing method just for the sake of it. I taught each method for the results I believed it would give my students. It was about the goal, not the means.

I'm guessing that you feel the same way. You don't care which swing method you follow, as long as you believe it will give you the results you want.

Well, what if I could show you there's an even faster and easier way to get results? What if I could show you that the best way to improve your swing is to stop following swing methods all together?

That's exactly what I'm going to do in this book. I'm going to show you how to get the results you want much more quickly and easily by approaching your golf swing from an entirely different direction.

Now There is a Better Way

This book will show you how to CUSTOM-FIT your golf swing. It is a completely different way to approach golf swing improvement – one that gives you the results you want more quickly and easily than any swing method ever could.

When you try to follow a swing method, you're always trying to learn someone else's way to swing. When you custom-fit your golf swing, you're always learning YOUR best swing – the only swing that fits you and your body perfectly.

This book will be different than any golf swing book you've ever read before. You won't find a generic, one-size-fits-all golf swing here, and I won't try to convince you that my version of the golf swing is the best swing method on the planet and the only truly "right way" to swing.

Instead, you will find something much more valuable – a simple, easy system to discover YOUR best way to swing!

Golf's First CUSTOM-FIT Swing Program

Year's ago, I promised myself that I would never write a book about the golf swing. With all the swing information already out there, I thought another golf swing book would be like pouring gasoline on the proverbial fire.

In the end though, that is exactly why I decided to write this book. I believe it is the first golf swing book that actually has a chance to help you put out that fire ... permanently!

If you have a chronic swing problem – like topping, slicing, or hooking – you can change it. If you have a specific swing goal – like increasing your consistency, distance, or accuracy – you can achieve it.

You can have all these things. And, you can have them all relatively quickly and easily. But, you can only have them by changing the way you currently approach your golf swing.

By the end of this book, you will know exactly what I mean. You will know how to have the golf swing you've always wanted. And, you will understand why it is so much faster and easier to improve your swing when you approach it from the direction of the *I-Swing System*.

The *I-Swing System* works for every golfer. It is the only program of its kind. Whether you are a new golfer or an experienced professional, whether you want to improve your swing a little or a lot, whether your body is in great condition or in need of an overhaul, the *I-Swing System* CUSTOM-FIT swing program will work for you.

The rewards are many. The direction is clear. All you need to decide now is – "How good do you want your swing to be?"

Dori O'Rourke
LPGA "Class A" Professional
San Diego, California

Chapter 1

There are Many Different Ways to Swing

Touring Pros Have Their Own Ways

Let's begin by establishing a very important point. There are many different ways to swing!

Jack Nicklaus is not only known for his amazing records, he's also recognized for his "flying right elbow." While being celebrated as one of the most popular golf professionals of all time, Nancy Lopez is also known for pre-setting her wrists at the start of her backswing. Annika Sorenstam is famous for having one of the most reliable golf swings ever. She's also known for turning her head to the target early in her forward swing.

No two golf swings are alike.

Famous Canadian golfer, Moe Norman, nicknamed "Pipeline Moe" for his uncanny accuracy, shot three 59's using an unconventional palm grip, a short backswing and very little hip rotation. Charlie Owens played with a cross-handed grip on the PGA Tour and Senior PGA Tour, where he won two events.

LPGA Hall-of-Famer, Amy Alcott, is known for her short backswing. LPGA Tour Star, Rosie Jones, is recognized by her flat backswing. PGA Tour Player, Jim Furyk, and Senior PGA Tour Players, Ray Floyd and Billy Casper, are known for extremely upright backswings.

Senior PGA Tour Players, Jim Thorpe and Allen Doyle, have each won numerous Senior PGA Tour events with very unconventional golf swings. The list of great players with atypical swings goes on and on.

Watch any professional golf tournament and you'll see that the best golfers in the world all swing differently. Some swings are more similar than others, but they all differ in some way. Just as no two people are exactly alike, no two golf swings are alike, either.

Teaching Pros Have Their Own Ways

No two golf instructors are alike, either. They believe in different ways to swing and consequently, they teach different swing techniques.

One golf professional may teach an overlapping grip, while another teaches interlocking. One may teach a narrow stance, while another teaches a wide stance. One may teach a flat backswing, while another teaches an upright backswing. And so on.

> # Hmmmm?
>
> If you take lessons from 10 different golf professionals, how many different ways to swing might you be shown?

With over 100 golf schools and 20,000 golf instructors in the United States alone, many different golf swings are being taught out there.

I've Taught Many Different Swings

I've been a golf instructor for over 20 years. During that time, I've had the great honor and privilege of working with over 5,000 men, women, juniors, and seniors; of all shapes, sizes, and skill levels. I've taught over 10,000 lessons, written two books, had over 100 golf magazine articles published, and presented well over 100 golf schools and mental game seminars across the country.

For the first 15 years of my teaching career, I've also taught many different golf swings. Motivated by my desire to help my students learn faster and to improve my own game, I studied everything I could find about the golf swing.

I watched videos, read magazines, attended seminars, and talked with other professionals; I studied the writings of famous tour players like Hogan, Nicklaus, and Runyan, and famous golf instructors like Toski, Ballard, and Flick.

With no shortage of information, I was constantly learning and trying new things. My swing beliefs shifted many times along the way. Of course, the swing I was teaching changed as well. Each time, I believed the new way was better than anything I had ever taught before.

In the beginning, you might say I taught more of a "conventional golf swing," although I used several different versions. In the middle, I taught what you might call an "athletic swing." In the end, I taught a method patterned after the swing of Moe Norman.

Several of the Swing Methods I've Taught

The following pages offer a quick look at some of the swing concepts and fundamentals that I've believed in and taught at various times in my career.

SETUP

Finger Positions on the Club

- Overlapping (photo 1-1)
- Interlocking (photo 1-2)
- 10-Finger "baseball style" (photo 1-3)

1-1

1-2

1-3

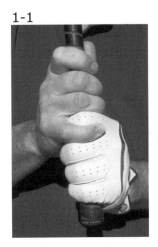

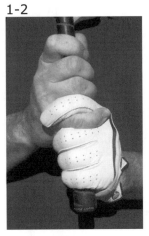

Overlapping
grip

Interlocking
grip

10-Finger
grip

Hand Positions on the Club

- Palms-facing, perpendicular to the target line –
  a "neutral" grip (photo 1-4)
- Palms-facing, hands rotated away from target –
  a "strong" grip (photo 1-5)
- Front hand "neutral" and back hand "strong" –
  (photo 1-6)

1-4
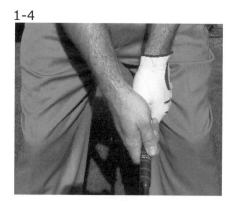

1-5
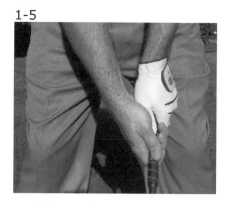

"Neutral" grip   "Strong" grip

1-6
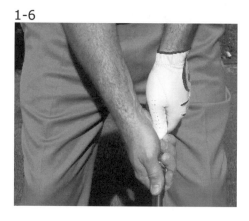

Front hand "neutral" and
back hand "strong"

What Do Front and Back Mean?

For the purposes of this book, I will refer to the hand, arm, shoulder, hip, leg, foot, and so on, that is on the side of the body *closest to the target* as the "front," and to the body parts on the side of the body *farthest from the target,* as the "back."

For example, if you are a right-handed golfer, your LEFT hand is your FRONT hand and your RIGHT hand is your BACK hand.

Using the terms "front" and "back" instead of "left" and "right" allows me to speak to both right and left-handed golfers at the same time.

Arm Positions

- Arms hang below shoulders (photo 1-7)
- Arms are extended in line with the club shaft (photo 1-8)

1-7   1-8

Arms hanging   Arms extended

Stance

- Shoulder-width
- Outside shoulder-width (wide)
- Less than shoulder-width with shorter clubs (narrow) and wider with longer clubs

Weight Distribution

- Weight evenly distributed on both feet
- More weight on the front foot to "anchor" the desired position at impact
- More weight on the back foot to get a "head start" on the backswing

Spine Tilt

- Spine vertical (photo 1-9)
- Spine tilted away from the target (photo 1-10)

1-9

1-10

Spine vertical

Spine tilted away from the target

BACKSWING

Initial Move

- One-piece takeaway, with shoulders, arms, and club starting back together
- Shoulder turn begins takeaway, arms and club follow
- Club begins takeaway, arms and shoulders follow

Angle Between Front Arm and Club Shaft

- Begins forming at the start of the backswing
- Begins forming when the club gets to waist height
- Forms naturally as the club swings back

Swing Plane

- Upright (photo 1-11)
- Flat (photo 1-12)

1-11

Upright swing plane

1-12

Flat swing plane

Top of Backswing

- Hands high, spine vertical (photo 1-13)
- Hands lower, spine tilted away from the target (photo 1-14)

1-13

1-14

Hands high,
spine vertical

Hands low,
spine tilted

FORWARD SWING

Transition Move

- Start by shifting weight to the front foot
- Start by letting the arms drop "into the slot"
- Start by turning the hips

Hip Position at Impact

- Clear the hips for power (photo 1-15)
- Square the hips for accuracy, with power (photo 1-16)

1-15

1-16

Hips rotated
approaching impact

Hips square
approaching impact

Finish Position

- Balanced on outside of front foot, spine tilted back – also called the "reverse C" position (photo 1-17)
- Balanced flat on front foot, spine vertical (photo 1-18)

1-17

1-18

Upper body tilted
at the finish

Upper body vertical
at the finish

If you think I've just shown you many different ways to swing, you ain't seen nothing yet! This is only the tip of the iceberg. There are literally hundreds of different swing methods I've read or heard about during my extensive study of the swing. If you are an avid student of the game, you probably have a sizeable list of your own!

Many Different Ways Work

Since many different swing methods are currently being taught, there certainly isn't just one right way. By watching the tour players, we can see there are many different ways to swing that work.

The fact is, for every aspect of the golf swing, there is a range of ways that works. For example:

A range of front hand positions ...

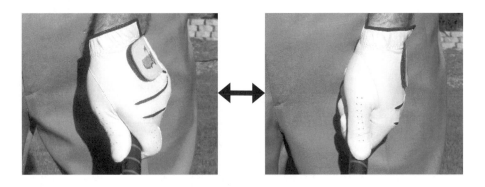

A range of back hand positions ...

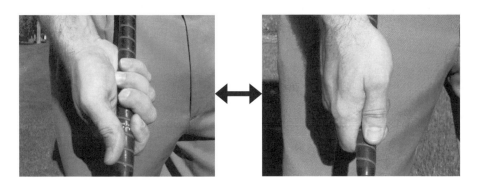

A range of different stances ...

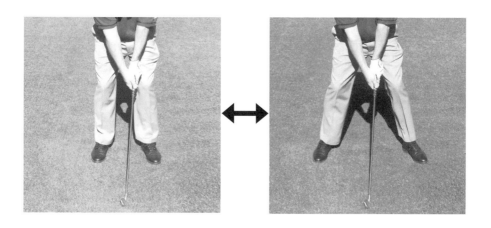

And, a range of effective swing planes ...

There are Many Different Ways to Swing   15

I'm sure there are golfers who even do things outside of these ranges and still get good results. For example, Charlie Owens's cross-handed full swing grip and Chris DiMarco's "claw" putting grip immediately come to mind.

This brings us back to the main point of this chapter – there are many different ways to swing. If you want to improve your swing in the fastest, easiest way, all you need to do is find the ONE that fits you best. By the end of this book, you will know exactly how to do that.

Next, I'm going to show you why all the swing methods in the world won't help you find YOUR best swing. It's time to break free from the swing method cycle!

Chapter 2

The Never-Ending Search

It Starts with the Grand Illusion

We know there are many different ways to swing, so the question is, "Which way is best for you?" That is the real question, isn't it? Well, for most golfers it's actually not, although it certainly ought to be!

The question that drives most golfers is, "What is the *right* way to swing?" New golfers, intermediate golfers, advanced golfers, and professional golfers all search for the answer to that same question. Every golf swing book you read, every swing video you watch, and every swing lesson you take is usually an attempt to find the answer.

What is the right way to hold the club? What is the right way to stand? How should I take the club back? Am I making the proper backswing? How should I shift my weight?

These seem like perfectly logical questions, and with so many golfers asking them it might be hard to see this at first, but there is a fundamental problem with the entire line of questioning. Can you see what it is?

You can only find the right way to swing if there *is* a right way to swing. In the last chapter, we just established the fact that there isn't. Therein lies the problem. When you're looking for the right way to swing, you are searching for something that doesn't exist. The right way to swing is an illusion.

The Grand Illusion ...

The belief there is one right way to swing.

Your Ideal Swing Combination

There isn't just one right way to swing, but there is one way to swing that is right for you. That is the swing you really need to be searching for – YOUR right way to swing.

Your right way to swing is different from everyone else's. It is a unique combination of setup, backswing, and forward swing motions and positions that come together perfectly to give you ultimate consistency, maximum distance, and pinpoint accuracy with ease.

Until you find your ideal swing combination, you will be plagued with inconsistency, inaccuracy, distance loss, and a swing that never feels exactly right.

When your golf swing doesn't fit you, it requires more energy, it causes your body unnecessary pain, and your brain continually fights it, trying to get back to a motion that is instinctively more comfortable.

So Many Swings, So Little Time

The reason you're still searching for your golf swing is that it's virtually impossible to find YOUR best swing in an ocean of swing methods, none of which were developed with your unique body in mind. All you're going to find are more and more *different* ways to swing.

> ### There isn't just one right way to swing, but there is one way to swing that is right for you.

Every Body is Different

No two bodies are alike. You may share some of the same physical characteristics with someone else, like height or weight, but as a whole your body is unique.

For example, bodies have different:

- Bone structure
- Musculature
- Flexibility
- Hip and shoulder width
- Arm and leg length
- Hand size
- Weight distribution
- Areas of tension
- Restrictions due to injury
- Strengths and weaknesses

If we expand our discussion to include the differences between each bone, joint, and muscle, the list above would increase exponentially.

If we include athletic backgrounds, movement patterns, degrees of balance, and so on, the differences would become even greater.

With all the physical differences between people, the same golf swing can't possibly work for every body.

Let's assume there are 10 setups, 10 backswings, and 10 forward swings that work. This results in 1,000 possible swing combinations (10 x 10 x 10).

If there are 1,000 possible swing combinations, then what you would be looking for is the one swing out of 1,000 that fits you best. In other words, the one setup, backswing, and forward swing combination that gives you the most power, consistency, and accuracy – that's YOUR right way to swing.

If only one swing fits you best, 999 of the 1,000 possible swing combinations are not right for you. Depending on the specific combination, each of the 999 would fall somewhere between "close to perfect" and "horribly miss-matched."

Most swing methods are offered as a package deal, meaning that the creators of the methods have taken their beliefs about the setup, backswing, and forward swing and packaged them together into one all-encompassing "swing method." Since your body is unique, it would take a real-life miracle for a pre-packaged swing method to fit you perfectly.

In most cases, part of it will fit you, and part of it won't. Consequently, when you leave one swing method to go looking for a better fit, the same problem will be awaiting you – parts of the new swing method will fit you, and other parts won't. The chance of you finding the perfect match is slim to none.

That is why you are still searching for your golf swing. You have been led to believe there is one right way to swing when there really isn't. You continue to search through an ever-growing mass of swing methods, hoping that the swing you want is right around the corner. But, try as you might, finding it is an impossible task.

When Will It End?

Imagine reading that an upright backswing is ideal for increasing your distance and consistency, so you decide to make your backswing more upright.

Then, a few weeks later, while watching golf on television, you hear a famous golf coach talking about the benefits of a flatter backswing. It worked for the winner of this week's tour event, so you figure it could work for you, too.

After a few weeks, you decide to take a lesson from the local professional. She explains that the best backswing is halfway between upright and flat, so you change again.

A few months later, a pro with a very upright backswing wins a big tour event. With your golf lesson a distant memory, you wonder if a flat backswing was your problem all along.

After months and months of backswing practice, you're no closer to finding YOUR best backswing than you were when you started.

With the ever-growing mass of swing information available today, this pattern could keep repeating with every aspect of your swing. When will it end?

15 Years of Searching Isn't Right!

I spent 15 years searching for the best way to swing. I didn't just study hundreds of books and videos, I also read every golf magazine I could find, attended numerous seminars and schools, and most importantly, I practiced.

I am actually one of those people who enjoys practicing. I had no problem hitting thousands and thousands of balls, driven by the belief that the new swing I was working on would be the last I would ever need to learn. It never was.

I am also what many people call a "natural athlete." I was an all-star softball player as a kid, tournament water skier as a teen, and scholarship tennis player in college. I took up soccer in my late 20's, ice hockey in my late 30's (barely knowing how to skate), and I now play in two weekly basketball leagues in my 40's. Sports had always come easily for me. So, what was the problem with golf?

I learned how to walk, run, swing a bat, throw a baseball, kick a soccer ball, and shoot a basketball with very little effort. I stopped "working on" those things years ago. Why, after 15 years, was I still searching for my golf swing?

How Long Have You Been Searching?

How many golf lessons have you taken? How many golf books and magazines have you read? How many golf swing videos have you watched? How much swing advice have you received from friends, family members, co-workers, playing partners, and strangers walking up to you on the range?

How many times have you been shown how to hold a club, how to stand, how to swing the club back, where to be at the top of your backswing, how to shift your weight, the proper path of your forward swing, the proper release, and so on?

If you're like most golfers, you have an abundance of information about the golf swing. Your mind is filled with swing tips and "how-to" information on every aspect of the swing.

Even when you're swinging well, though, you wonder if there's a better way. There is always a question mark, always a temptation to try something new.

If you already knew you had the best swing for your body, you could be done learning about the swing and your search would be over. Instead, you search on and on.

How Many Different Swing Combinations Are There?

When you count all the different aspects of setup, backswing, and forward swing (grip, stance, spine tilt, takeaway, swing plane, shoulder turn, weight shift, etc.) and all the possible ways each can be done (the range for each aspect), there are well over 1,000,000 different swing combinations.

Do the math for yourself. To keep it simple, pretend there are only 10 different ways to do each aspect of the swing, and use only the 7 aspects listed above – 10 grips x 10 stances x 10 spine tilts x 10 takeaways x 10 swing planes x 10 shoulder turns x 10 weight shifts. That equals 10,000,000 swing combinations!

Golf swing methods continue to come and go like clothing styles. As the popularity of the world's top players and coaches changes, the latest "best way to swing" trend changes with them.

With so many conflicting ideas, you're constantly having to decide who you should believe.

- This year's leading money winner?
- The professional you just saw on television?
- The author of the most recent golf article you read?
- Tiger Woods' coach? (His last one or his current one?)
- The best player you know?

There will always be another swing method marketing itself as "the best." There will always be another best-selling book or video. As long as you continue to look for your golf swing in this mountain of swing advice, you will forever be stuck in a never-ending cycle.

Q and A

"What is the right way to swing?"

"It depends on who you ask."

Are You Ready to End Your Search?

"What am I doing wrong?" "Am I standing the right way?" "Why can't I be consistent?" If you've been asking these same questions for as long as you've been playing golf, does that concern you?

What is it you still think you're missing? What new thing do you hope to discover every time you pick up a golf magazine or swing method book?

It's the same pool of information, and you're asking the same questions over and over. You may even feel like you're getting somewhere because you're gathering more and more information. But, did you ever notice that you keep ending up right back where you started, still asking yourself the same question you had when you first took up golf: "What is the right way to swing?"

Take a good look at all the swing information out there because this massive collection of swing tips, swing keys, and "secrets" is where you keep looking for your golf swing. You haven't found it there yet, but you keep looking for it in the exact same place, hoping that something new will somehow magically appear.

I call this the "swing method" approach. You've been unknowingly stuck in it since the first day someone showed you how to swing. Are you ready to finally break free?

Chapter 3

You've Been Going in the Wrong Direction

Two Distinctly Different Approaches

You already know about the swing method approach. That's when you take a pre-determined way to swing and you do your best to learn it. You're probably also well aware of the confusing contradictions, awkward, uncomfortable swing motions, and other problems normally associated with that approach.

Custom-fitting your golf swing is an entirely different way to approach swing improvement. Instead of starting with a specific swing method in mind, you start with the most important aspect of your swing.

A CUSTOM-FIT golf swing starts by focusing on the one aspect of your swing that directly determines what happens to your golf shot. This guarantees you'll get the results you want. It's also the secret to improving your swing in the fastest, easiest way possible.

The Most Important Aspect of Your Swing

"What is the most important aspect of your golf swing?" I've asked that question to hundreds of golfers across the United States and I've heard a wide variety of answers – everything from grip and alignment, to backswing and tempo, just to name a few.

The fact is only ONE aspect of your golf swing is MOST important. To find it, you need to look for the one thing that must be present to hit a good golf shot. There are a lot of things that might help, but there is only one thing that DIRECTLY causes the results of your shots.

If we were on a driving range together when I asked you that question, I'd have a little fun disproving your answers until you were able to figure it out for yourself.

For example, if you answered that "grip" was the most important aspect of the golf swing, I would take a really bizarre-looking grip and hit a solid, straight shot. If you said that "stance" was the most important, I might stand with both my feet turned away from the target, or I might stand on one leg. Either way, I'd hit a solid, straight shot.

In other words, I would take whatever answer you gave me and demonstrate that it's possible to hit a nice, straight shot in a completely different way than what you believe is right.

Or, conversely, I would correctly use what you said was the most important aspect of the swing, yet hit a grounder or shank. For example, if you thought "stance" was most important, I would set up in what you consider to be the perfect stance and purposefully top or shank the ball.

I'll do this with every answer you give me until you hone in on the only answer I can't prove wrong. Since I can take an awkward, pretzel-like backswing and still hit a good shot, then "backswing" can't be it. Since I can even take a beautifully smooth, picture-perfect swing and top the ball, "swinging smoothly" can't be the answer either.

Ultimately, there is only one thing that MUST happen for you to hit a good golf shot – your club must connect with the ball properly at impact!

IMPACT is without a doubt the most important aspect of your golf swing. It is the ONLY thing that directly determines the results of your shots. Everything else is secondary.

> **IMPACT is the most important aspect of your golf swing. Everything else is secondary.**

The Only Thing That Really Matters

When you want to improve your golf swing, what you really need to improve is your impact. It doesn't matter how many swing changes you make, if you're not changing the one thing that matters most, you won't see the results you want.

The only thing that actually matters about your golf swing is how your club and ball connect at impact. The ball doesn't care how you set up or what kind of backswing you made. All it cares about are the forces applied to it by your golf club.

You could spend a month practicing your backswing. You could develop the ideal tempo. You could even do your best to make your golf swing look exactly like the swing of your favorite touring pro. But, if the leading edge of your golf club connects with the top of the ball at impact, you're going to hit a grounder. Your golf ball doesn't care a bit about how your swing looks!

Swing methods are more focused on how you look. However, whether they are similar or differ greatly from one another, ultimately every swing method is intended for the same purpose – to get you to the same place.

All touring professionals have their own unique ways to swing, but they all do one thing exactly the same – SOLID IMPACT!

IMPACT!

"The Moment of Truth"

Impact is that place. It's the top dog. It's the one thing you MUST have to get the results you want. How you do it – the swing method you use – is secondary.

The Solid Foundation You Need

Impact isn't just the most important aspect of your golf swing; it's also the key that will free you from the never-ending cycle of swing methods.

The only way you will ever stop circling from one swing method to the next is to build your swing on a rock solid foundation. You need a constant – something that won't change over time.

Impact is that constant. Impact is the same now as it has always been. It doesn't vary with the season. It doesn't change from coach to coach. It has never changed and it never will. It will always be there for you.

A swing method isn't right or wrong just because someone says it is. A swing method is right or wrong based on how well it allows YOU to get your club where it needs to be at impact.

For example, if you want to know whether a flat backswing or an upright backswing is better, the answer is simple. It's the one that makes it easier for you to swing your club into the ideal position at impact.

You've Got to Know Why!

A little girl was watching her mom prepare to cook a ham. She saw her mom cut the ends off the ham and place it into a pan. "Mom, why do you cut the ends off the ham?" she asked.

Her mother thought about it for a moment and said, "You know, Honey, I'm not sure why. I guess I do it because my mother did it. Why don't you call your grandmother and ask her?"

So, the little girl called her grandmother and asked her the same question. "Grandma, why do you cut the ends off a ham before cooking it? Mom told me she couldn't remember why she does it except that she watched you do it."

The little girl's grandmother gave it some thought, then said, "Darling, after all these years, I really can't tell you why either. I guess I do it for the same reason as your mother – because I saw my mother do it."

Luckily the little girl's great grandmother was still alive, so she called her next. "Great Grandmother, Mom told me she cuts the end off the ham before putting it in the pan because Grandmother did. And, Grandma said she cuts the ends off the ham because you did. So, why do you cut the ends off the ham before cooking it?"

The little girl could hear her great grandmother laughing out loud.

After a few moments, great grandmother composed herself and said, "I'm so sorry for laughing, Honey, but the thought of my daughter and granddaughter wasting ham all these years amuses me. I cut the ends off the ham years ago because it was too big to fit in the oven pan!"

Lesson to Be Learned: Don't waste time and money following swing advice without knowing exactly how it will improve your impact.

An Entirely Different Direction

A CUSTOM-FIT golf swing starts at impact. It's the most important aspect of your swing and the one thing you MUST have to get the results you want, so it's the most logical place to begin.

Starting at impact means you start with the moment of truth and work back from there. It means you understand exactly what has to happen between the club and ball at impact to get the results you want. It means you focus on the position of your golf club first, before ever thinking about your body.

Which Color is Better – Blue or Green?

"Better for what?" To objectively make a choice between blue and green you would need more information. For example, if your goal is to paint a picture of the sky, then blue is the better color. If your goal is to paint a picture of grass, then green is the better color.

The same is true for golf swings. If you want to know which swing method is better, you need to ask, "Better for what?"

Just as the colors blue and green are equally good until they have a purpose, swing methods are equally good until you relate them to impact. Once you do that, it's easy to know which one is best.

Once you understand that your body motions are secondary to impact, then choosing to follow a swing program that starts with a specific swing method in mind makes absolutely no sense.

It's like getting into a car and driving with no idea where you're going. It's like putting the cart before the horse, the caboose in front of the engine, the 19th hole before the … well, you have the idea!

The Only Way that Guarantees Results

Starting at impact is the fastest, easiest way to get the results you want and it's the only way to guarantee them. A change to your setup or your backswing doesn't guarantee a change to your club position at impact, but focusing directly on your club does.

For example, if your problem is topping the ball, you could bend your head down to your waist and keep your front arm as straight as a board. Even so, you might still top the ball when you swing.

On the other hand, if you focus directly on your club and make sure it connects solidly with the ball, you'll see immediate results. Guaranteed. Every time.

As you will see in the next chapter, starting at impact is a completely different way to approach swing improvement. And, it's the secret to finding YOUR best swing!

Two Completely Different Approaches, Only One That Guarantees Results

Swing Method Approach – the focus is on your body, with the hope it will have a positive affect on your impact – the direction is from your body DOWN to impact.

CUSTOM-FIT Swing Approach – the focus is on impact, with the guarantee that it will give you the results you want – the direction is from impact UP to your body.

Chapter 4

A Completely Different Approach

Start with Impact

Swing methods can be helpful, but like prescription drugs they can also have harmful side affects. They can lead to confusing contradictions, physical discomfort, and a search that never ends.

A CUSTOM-FIT golf swing starts with impact. Results are immediate and guaranteed, and you completely bypass all the problems normally associated with swing methods. You find YOUR best swing quickly and easily.

I call this approach the "I-Swing System." The "I" in "I-Swing" stands for "Instinctive." Your Instinctive Swing is YOUR best swing. It is your body's easiest, most powerful, and most comfortable way to reach the ideal impact position.

Instinctive (in-stingk'tiv)

Innate; natural; spontaneous; inherent; unthinking; intuitive

---

A Life-Changing Realization

After 15 years of going from one swing method to the next, searching for my swing, I felt I had done everything humanly possible to find it, but I still didn't have the swing I wanted.

All the different swing methods, all the long hours of practice, all to no avail. I was frustrated and disillusioned, to say the least.

It was a time in my life when I felt like I'd hit rock bottom. It wasn't a good feeling, and I wanted it to go away. But, it didn't. And, as it turned out, that was a good thing. Now, when I look back on this time in my life, I realize its significance.

Hitting bottom jarred me from my normal way of thinking long enough to step back and see things from a different perspective. I let go of knowing. My mind opened.

That's when it hit me. There is one thing every swing method strives to achieve. There is one goal they all share in common. What if I just started there?

Of course, that one thing is impact, and that is exactly where I started. I gave myself very specific instructions. I had permission to swing any way I wanted as long as my club ended up in the correct position at impact.

Total Freedom

What joy! What delight! What freedom! For the first time in my life, my body was in charge, not my head. The only guideline was to make sure my club ended up in the proper position at impact. Other than that, I was totally free to do whatever I wanted.

That's when the real fun began. If you're free to swing any way you want, how are you going to swing? Are you going to choose a difficult, awkward, uncomfortable motion, or are you going to choose the easiest and most comfortable way?

Instead of struggling to swing the "right way," I had an exciting new mission – to find the easiest, most powerful, and most comfortable way to swing for MY body.

If It Feels Good, Do It!

For the first time since I started playing golf, it was all about me. What felt good to me? There were no rights or wrongs, and there was no one telling me what I should or shouldn't do. I gave myself total permission to swing any way I wanted. Ahhhh, glorious freedom!

To find YOUR body's best way to swing, you need to shift your focus from trying to swing the "right way," to finding the swing that feels best to you, too.

It's time to base your swing on the setup positions and swing motions that feel best for YOUR body. You are in charge. You are the judge. You finally have a rock solid way to know which swing is truly right for YOU!

This is my favorite part of the I-Swing System because it allows you to find YOUR best swing – your Instinctive Swing.

After 15 long years of searching, I can hardly put into words how unbelievably awesome it felt to find MY best swing! My search is over and yours will be too!

What If What Feels Good is WRONG?

When you read the heading, "If It Feels Good, Do It," did you suddenly break into a sweat? Did the hairs on the back of your neck stand up? Did your stomach begin to churn?

Does the idea of having a swing that feels good strike fear into your heart? If so, always remember that impact, not a swing method, determines the results of your shots.

Could Wrong Be Right?

As a new golf professional, I noticed that many golfers, especially women, preferred a "strong" grip (photo 4-1).

At the time, I believed that the right way to hold the club was to have a "neutral" grip. Therefore, I would correct my students and show them the "right way."

4-1

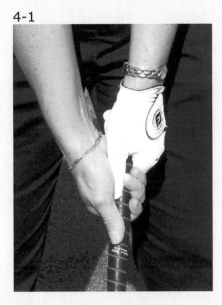

I remember thinking how strange it was that so many people seemed to naturally put their hands in the wrong position.

A "strong" grip

Experience is a great teacher, though.

Now I think it's even stranger that I was so locked into a swing method. I didn't even consider the possibility that many people used a strong grip because it was the best way for them to hold the club!

When impact is ideal, you'll get the power, consistency, and accuracy you want. Therefore, as long as you accomplish that, having a good-feeling swing can't be wrong.

The key is to start with impact. With the I-Swing System, you don't just haphazardly do what feels good. Your club at impact is your anchor and your guiding light. It's your port in the swing method storm.

FIRST, you make sure your club is in the proper position at impact. THEN, you find your body's easiest way to get it there. What could be more right than that?

Trust Yourself to Know What's Right

Deciding what feels best to you might be a new idea for golf, but it's something you've been doing your whole life. Feeling the difference between any two swing methods is similar to feeling the difference between any two pairs of shoes, pants, or gloves. You simply choose the one that fits you best.

A Simple Shift of Focus

If your mind is focused on swinging the "right way," you will force your body to do whatever you believe is right, no matter how awkward or uncomfortable.

If your mind is focused on getting your club into the ideal position at impact, in the easiest and most comfortable way, you're guaranteed great results and a swing that feels great, too!

Who Really Knows Best?

Kids sometimes pick up golf clubs and hold them with reverse or split-hand grips. A reverse grip is when the back hand is above the front hand, opposite of how golfers normally hold clubs. In a split-hand grip, the hands are spread apart, similar to the way hockey players hold sticks (photo 4-2).

4-2

Junior golfer with a split-hand grip

One of the first things golf professionals and well-meaning adults do when a child has a split-hand grip is put the child's hands in the "proper position." They take the bottom hand and slide it back up the club so the two hands are touching. I used to do this too ... until I met the GIANT golf club.

(continued from previous page)

I was at a pro shop and saw a giant golf club on display. It was about 9 feet long, with a head about a foot wide and a shaft the size of a 1-inch diameter PVC pipe.

I thought it would be fun to pick up the giant club and imagine using it to drive the ball a mile. So, I placed my hands on the grip the same way I always do, and I started to set up to my imaginary golf ball. The giant club was so heavy, though, I couldn't lift it.

Then, without even thinking about it, my body made a simple adjustment and the club lifted right up.

Suddenly, I realized what happened. I had instinctively gone to a split-hand grip, slipping my hand down the shaft, "hockey-style," to create the leverage I needed to pick up the heavy club. Years of showing junior golfers the "right way" to hold a club came rushing to my mind.

Was a split-hand grip a child's intuitive way of picking up a heavy golf club? How many times had I tried to teach the "right way" to hold a club, against a child's natural instincts?

Now I believe that the children who kept returning to the way that felt good, no matter how many times I tried to show them the "right way," were already listening to the best teachers they had ... their own bodies!

As a golfer, you may have been told things like:

- The golf swing is an unnatural movement.
- If it feels good, you're not doing it right.
- If your swing feels awkward or uncomfortable, it is probably right.
- Don't worry about how bad it feels, you'll get used to it.
- If you want to swing the right way, do the opposite of what you think you should do.

The underlying message of these beliefs is to disregard how your swing feels and focus on doing it "right." Well, we already know where that road leads!

Nobody wants to swing the wrong way. And, most of us are told from very early on, that left to our own devices, our golf swings will go terribly astray. However, that's not true when you start with the golf club at impact and you work back from there.

Finding your best swing can be an absolute joy. The process is simple. There are fewer things to think about. Learning is fun. The results are immediate. You'll be more consistent. You'll hit longer, straighter shots. And, your swing will feel great ... which will make your body very happy!

Your best swing is different from everyone else's. No swing method matches it. You'll never find it in a book or DVD, and no one can teach it to you. You're the only one who knows exactly what it is because you are the only one who knows what FEELS BEST to your body.

The more you release your Instinctive Swing, the better your swing will be. Improvement is guaranteed, so there's no limit to how far you can go. The only thing you need to decide is, "How good do I want my swing to be?"

It's time to find out.

Trust Yourself

With impact handled first, the swing that FEELS BEST to YOU is the RIGHT way to swing!

Chapter 5

How Good Do You Want to Be?

The Stage is Set

In Chapter 1, I wanted you to understand that there are many different ways to swing.

In Chapter 2, I wanted you to understand why going from one swing method to the next won't bring you any closer to YOUR best swing.

In Chapter 3, I wanted you to understand that impact is the most important aspect of your swing and therefore, the most logical starting point for swing improvement.

In Chapter 4, I wanted you to understand that the swing that feels best to you is the right way to swing.

The first four chapters have set the stage for the rest of this book by focusing on the reasons why custom-fitting your golf swing makes sense. The remainder of this book will cover the actual nuts and bolts of the I-Swing System.

This chapter serves as the "turning point" – the transition from the underlying principles to hands-on application. This is where you will decide just how good you want your swing to be.

How Your Golf Swing Fits In

There is more to your golf game than just your swing. When you want to improve your *game*, your golf swing is only one piece of the pie (for our purposes here, "golf swing" refers to your full swing, short game, and putting strokes).

Although the golf swing gets most of the attention, it's actually not as big a piece of the pie as you might think.

For example, here are 25+ areas you could also choose to improve for the benefit of your game:

- Presence/State of Mind
- Focus and Concentration
- Pre and Post-Shot Routines
- Management of Your Emotions
- Attitude and Motivation
- Self-Trust/Intuition
- Self-Worth/Self-Esteem
- Creativity and Visualization
- Course Management
- Specialty Shots
- Relaxation
- Feel for Distance
- Practice Effectiveness
- Fitness and Nutrition
- Strength and Flexibility
- Rules and Etiquette
- Shoes and Clothing
- Clubs and Equipment

How important each of these areas is to your overall golf improvement is based on your personal goals and a current assessment of your game.

For example, if your number one goal is lowering your score, the area of your game that is costing you the most strokes would rank the highest.

Personalized Improvement Plans

If I was your personal coach, the first thing I would do is help you clarify what you want. Why do you play golf? What do you enjoy most about golf? What would you envision for the future of your golf game if you knew you could reach your true potential?

Once you were clear about your most important goals, then we would discuss how much time you're willing to invest toward those goals.

> ### A "Personalized Improvement Plan" is the WHAT and HOW of golf improvement.

With clear goals and a realistic evaluation of your time, we would create a "Personalized Improvement Plan" (PIP) – a map that shows you the best way to get from where you are to where you want to be.

A Personalized Improvement Plan gives you the two things you need to guarantee steady progress – WHAT to do and HOW to do it. You MUST know these two things before ever going out to practice or play.

By the end of this book, you will know how to create a Personalized Improvement Plan for your *golf swing* – a map that will show you the fastest, easiest way to take your swing from where it is now to where you want it to be.

Although it is outside the scope of this book, once you've become more familiar with this process, it will be even more effective to create future Personalized Improvement Plans that take your "whole game" into account.

This Stuff Really Works

Whether you believe it now or not, your golf swing will absolutely get where you want it to be, as long as you continue following the I-Swing System. Your swing will keep getting better and better, and that's a guarantee.

It's guaranteed because you will start with impact – the moment of truth in your golf swing. From there, you will learn how to make it easier and easier for your body to get your club into the ideal impact position.

Impact will give you the results you want; and the better your swing feels, the more power, accuracy, and consistency you will have. It's that simple.

When you know something works, you don't have to "give it a try," you simply need to commit to mastering it. The I-Swing System works. So, your golf swing can actually be as good as your time allows. You just need to decide how good you want it to be.

Your Swing, Your Choice

I know we're just getting started, so this isn't a decision you'll probably make any time soon, but I think it's important to keep the following in mind.

At any point, you can decide that your golf swing is good enough just as it is. Instead of choosing to improve your swing, you can choose to fully enjoy your game without ever putting another minute into swing improvement.

> **You don't have to work on your swing for as long as you play golf!**

As I discussed in an earlier chapter, I love to play soccer, basketball, and ice hockey. Except for my occasional research project, like when I decided to see what I could learn from changing my free throw shot routine, I don't practice any of those three sports any more.

It's not because I can't get better; I know I most definitely could. It's because I've decided that I'm good enough just as I am. I am completely happy and content playing those sports at my current skill level. I love playing in weekly league games and tournaments, but I don't choose to put any more time or effort into practice.

At any point along the way, you can decide that your golf game is good enough as it is, too. You can choose to fully enjoy the game and the swing you have.

Enjoy Your Game Fully ... Now!

Assuming that you plan to keep improving for at least a few more months, it also makes sense to enjoy the game you have WHILE you continue to improve.

Many golfers believe they can't enjoy golf until their game reaches a certain level. The truth is, your skill level and your enjoyment of the game are not locked together.

> **You can enjoy the game you have WHILE improving your swing.**

There are many people who enjoy swimming without being world-class swimmers, and I enjoy ice hockey despite the fact that my teammates can skate circles around me – literally!

You don't have to shoot par and you don't need a perfect swing to enjoy golf. Regardless of your skill level, you can enjoy the game 100% right now.

Many golfers say, "If I could just break 100, then I'd be happy." If you've said that before, what happened when you broke 100? Were you happy?

Of course you were. However, when the excitement died down, did your happiness then depend on breaking 90? Then what?

Do You Doubt Continual Improvement?

You may have a history of investing time and money on swing changes that haven't produced the results they promised. If so, it's time to put that doubt aside.

Remember, when you're trying to follow a swing method, there's no guarantee the changes you're making with your BODY will positively affect your CLUB position at impact.

However, there is a guarantee you'll get the results you want when you focus directly on your club at impact.

With the I-Swing System, you will know exactly what changes you need to make, and upon completion, they will lead to the results you want.

Continual improvement is not just a possibility; it's a guarantee. So, go for it! You can do it!

If you're not enjoying golf with your current swing, what makes you think you'll enjoy it any more with a different swing?

With the I-Swing System, you have the opportunity for continual improvement for as long as you play golf. So, don't wait until you "get there" to fully enjoy the game.

It's your swing, your game, and your life. You decide how good you want to be. And, you can choose to enjoy the game WHILE improving your swing!

Congratulations on your decision to improve. With the stage completely set, let me show you the first thing you can do TODAY to see an immediate improvement in your swing.

Chapter 6

Your Swing is Better Than You Think

The Fastest Way to Immediate Improvement

I hope you have your swimsuit handy because it's time to dive in! I'm going to show you exactly what you can do to improve your golf swing IMMEDIATELY.

Based on my experience coaching thousands of golfers over the past 20+ years, I have discovered the fastest way to see an immediate improvement in your swing. The secret is to *optimize it*.

There are two distinctly different ways to improve your golf swing. You can:

1. *Optimize* your swing habit
2. *Change* your swing habit

Optimizing your swing habit means making the most of your current swing mechanics. In other words, improving your golf swing without making any changes to your grip, stance, takeaway, shoulder turn, weight shift, or any of the other mechanics of your swing.

The best way to optimize your swing is to improve your mental state, smoothness, tempo, balance, or relaxation. For example, if you improve your swing tempo, you will see an immediate improvement in your swing, even though you still have the same swing mechanics you had when you started.

> # The fastest way to improve your swing is to OPTIMIZE it!

In contrast, *changing* your swing habit means changing the physical mechanics of your swing. For example, changing any of the things I mentioned above – like grip, stance, takeaway, and so on.

When you *optimize* your swing, you are improving your swing as a "whole." When you make a swing *change*, you are changing a "part" of your swing.

The biggest difference between optimizing your swing and changing it is the amount of time each change requires. Any time invested in swing optimization is helpful, whereas, a time commitment of three weeks to one year is often required before you will see consistent results from a change to your mechanics.

Changes to your setup normally take the shortest amount of time – from three weeks to a month to complete, while changes to your backswing or forward swing usually take the longest – from one to several months to complete.

Swing Optimization	vs.	Swing Change
Better use of CURRENT mechanics	vs.	NEW swing mechanics
Improve your WHOLE swing	vs.	Change a PART of your swing
MINIMAL time commitment required	vs.	3 weeks to 1 year time commitment required

When I say, "complete", I mean that you "own" the new swing mechanic. In other words, it happens automatically, without thought, and under stress, just like your current swing habit.

"Owning a change" is the ultimate goal of a swing change because it means the change will show up on the course without conscious thought.

Most golfers spend the majority of their time trying to *change* their swings. They are constantly tinkering with their setup or testing out the latest tip. Rarely is any time dedicated to swing optimization.

Whether you are a recreational golfer, weekly club player, or touring professional, you would be better off spending the majority of your practice time on swing optimization. At a minimum, you should devote at least half of your practice to it.

Optimize Your Swing Before Changing It

As we just discussed, changing a swing habit takes time ... often a LOT of time! From the moment you decide to make a change, until the time you "own" that change, can take from three weeks to a year, depending on how often, and more importantly, how effectively you practice.

If you start a swing change and you don't complete it, you'll revert back to your old habit and have nothing to show for your time. However, when you optimize your swing, you'll get an immediate pay off from any quality time you invest.

So, time is one reason it's smart to optimize your swing before deciding to change it. Another simple reason to optimize your swing first is ... your swing is better than you think!

No, I'm not crazy. If you're like the vast majority of golfers I've known, you've just been so busy trying to change your swing, you can't possibly know how good it is.

Is Your Golf Swing a Habit?

I've presented numerous mental game seminars through the years. One of my favorite questions to ask the audience is, "Do you think your golf swing is a habit?"

Very few golfers ever answer, "Yes." When I ask why, the most frequent response is, "If my golf swing was a habit, my results wouldn't be so inconsistent!"

That's when I say, "Imagine that three golfers who you play golf with regularly are standing behind a screen. The screen prevents you from recognizing one from the other, but you can see a silhouette of each person swinging. Based just on their golf swing, can you tell them apart?"

"Yes, of course!" is the immediate response.

To that I reply, "Even if the results of their shots are inconsistent, the overall swing motion is the same from one swing to the next. That's because each golfer's swing is a habit … just like yours."

If you've played golf for more than a month, YOUR golf swing is a habit, too! So, treat it accordingly by optimizing it or scheduling the time required to change it.

The problem is this: When you try to change your swing, you consciously interfere with it. When you consciously interfere with it, you block your swing habit from showing up. When you block it from showing up, your swing feels worse than it is.

> # Ever Wish You Could Just Hit the Ball With Your Practice Swing?
>
> If your practice swing is better than your ball swing, it proves your golf swing is better than you think.
>
> Until you can take your practice swing to the ball, you don't need to change your swing mechanics, you need to optimize your swing!

If you think your *worst* swings represent your real swing habit, you will constantly want to change your swing, and back to the top of the loop you'll go.

Until you allow your real swing habit to show up, you're just trying to change your worst swings over and over again. To see your real swing habit, you need to look at your *best* swings.

Will Your Real Swing Habit Please Stand Up

The first thing I recommend you do to optimize your swing is stop thinking about it when you play. Play golf the same way you would throw a baseball to first base – see the target and throw – with no thoughts about "how."

Picture yourself teeing off with no swing thoughts of any kind – a quiet mind, totally focused on the target. See yourself watching the shot fly through the air, land, and come to a stop, without any comments about what you did wrong or what you need to do to fix your swing for the next shot.

The Tortoise and the Hare - A Golf Improvement Story

Let's say you have one hour to practice this week and you decide to spend it trying out the new takeaway you read about in the latest golf magazine. Your golf buddy decides to spend his hour practicing his tempo (i.e., optimizing his current swing habit).

The next week, you spend your hour of practice trying out a new grip. Your golf buddy practices his tempo again.

The following week, you decide that your club path is wrong, so you work on that. Your buddy practices his tempo some more.

How much swing improvement will you each have at the end of those three weeks? Your swing will be exactly the same, or worse. Your golf buddy, on the other hand, will enjoy a great deal of improvement.

That's because you somehow tricked yourself into believing that one hour of practice dabbling on your takeaway, grip, and club path could result in a permanent change.

Your golf buddy knew better. He practiced one thing consistently and saw a real improvement in his tempo, which rewarded him with lower scores, greater accuracy, and more consistency.

How different would it be to give up conscious control over your swing? How much more fun would it be to let go and play? Wouldn't it be relaxing to just choose your target, step up to your ball, and swing?

You Can Free Your Mind from Swing Thoughts

If you're one of those very rare golfers who can play a round of golf without a commentary about your swing running through your head, you may think this is not a big deal. But for most golfers, playing golf without thinking about their swings seems nearly impossible.

The vast majority of golfers believe their swing thoughts, like security blankets, keep horrible things from happening. Without them, they may even envision themselves standing frozen over the ball, unable to swing at all.

Since most golfers have developed the habit of playing golf while thinking about their swing, the idea of letting your swing just "be" is probably a strange and foreign concept. It might even be a little scary.

I've been in that boat, and I can tell you it was quite scary for me. Thinking about my golf swing gave me a sense of security and control that I liked and didn't want to lose.

Deep down, however, I knew that letting go of that control was my best hope for improvement. This became even more apparent when I realized that golf was the ONLY sport where I thought about my mechanics while playing.

Knowing that, I stopped thinking about my golf swing "cold turkey," went out on the course the next day, and never thought about my swing again. NOT!

Are Your Swing Mechanics Really the Problem?

Imagine walking along a balance beam that is resting flat on the ground. Then, imagine walking along that balance beam again – only this time it's placed between the rooftops of two, 10-story buildings. What changes might you experience?

You walked perfectly fine when the balance beam was on the ground. However, now that it's raised 10 stories into the air, your walking is much different. Instead of gliding confidently and effortlessly across the beam, now you are taking painfully slow, tentative, jerky steps.

Here's the big question: If I'm your balance beam coach and my job is to improve the way you walk on the balance beam when it's between the two rooftops, what should I focus on during your practice time? Should I spend the time trying to change the way you walk, or should I focus on something else?

If we spend time trying to change your walking habit, you won't see improvement because that's not the real problem. The problem is what changed in your mind when the balance beam was placed in the air.

Similarly, you shouldn't spend time trying to change your swing just because it doesn't show up on the golf course if it's perfectly fine in a practice swing or on the range!

If you can stop thinking about your golf swing cold turkey, more power to you. For me, it was a process. Even though I knew that thinking about my mechanics in other sports interfered with my performance, I didn't just go out on the course the next day and play free of swing thoughts.

The other sports gave me the proof that I would play better if I stopped thinking about my swing. They opened my mind to see there was a better way to play. Most importantly, they gave me a working model that I used to guide my golf game back to a more natural state.

If you've played other sports, you can also use them as reference points. They can be the perfect examples of how well you can play without consciously thinking about the mechanics of your motion.

If you haven't played many sports in your life, that's not a problem. Just look at some of the things you perform in everyday life that you don't have to think about, like walking, driving a car, throwing a wad of paper into the trash, brushing your teeth, and putting your shoes on. You don't consciously control those movements, and yet you do them just fine.

Hurry! Your Golf Swing is Waiting!

Can you hear that? It's your golf swing screaming to be set free. It's been trapped for what feels like an eternity. It desperately wants you to know that LETTING GO is the key.

Don't allow your real swing habit to stay buried under all those swing thoughts that keep running through your head. Take my challenge and allow your real swing to come out in all its glory.

Your First BIG Challenge

Here is your mission should you decide to accept it:
The next 5 times you go to a driving range, and the next
5 times you go to the course, accept the swing you have.
Pick a target, swing, and watch where the ball goes.
Then, repeat the process.

Feel free to notice what is happening when you swing, but
don't try to control it, change it, or fix it in any way.

You play baseball without thinking about the way you
throw, soccer without thinking about the way you kick,
and basketball without thinking about the way you shoot.
Therefore, your brain is fully capable of hitting a golf ball
without your conscious interference.

So, choose a target, step up to the ball, and swing. If you
miss-hit a shot, trust your brain to make the necessary
adjustments, and move on.

This is a process. Just do your best to stay on task and
notice what happens as a result. For example, how often
do you catch yourself thinking about your swing? When
is the urge the strongest? And so on.

Consider your mission a success if you simply stick with
the process for your next 5 range visits and next 5
rounds of golf. Enjoy!

The first step is to stop thinking about your swing when you play. Once you can consistently do that, the next step is to learn how to take your best practice swing to the ball.

The process I developed for this is called, "The Miracle Swing Change Process." In the next chapter, you'll learn how quickly the process works, and you'll understand why the name fits perfectly.

Chapter 7

The Miracle Swing Change Process

Your Golf Swing Isn't the Problem

We all remember significant events in our lives like our first kiss, first car, first hole-in-one, and so on. Well, I'll always remember the first golf lesson I gave using the *Miracle Swing Change Process*.

I didn't call it that back then and it's evolved through the years. But, I knew it was something special the first day it "magically" appeared in my mind.

Early in my career, I realized that golfers could have perfectly good golf swing habits in their brains, and then unfortunately, interfere with them to the degree that it looked like they didn't know how to swing at all.

Conscious interference is really a mental issue, but most golfers believe their golf swings are the problem. As a result, they focus their efforts on trying to fix their swings. The more they try to fix their swings, the worse they become, which makes them even more determined. Inevitably, a vicious cycle develops.

Soon, they can't hit the broad side of a barn, and out of desperation they call the local golf professional for help. That's exactly what happened to a woman I'll call Sammy – an avid golfer with an 18-handicap.

Sammy's Story

Sammy came to me terribly distraught and ready to quit golf forever. "I've lost my swing," she said, shaking her head in despair. "I can't even hit the ball in the air anymore!"

I asked her to take a few swings so I could see just how "lost" her swing actually was. She topped balls, shanked them, popped them up, and after every shot, she said something to the effect of, "See, I told you."

Sammy wasn't lying. Her swing was nowhere to be found! Luckily, I realized that her swing wasn't really gone; it was just buried beneath a pile of swing thoughts and negative feelings. I knew my job was to help her uncover it.

Sammy told me about the long list of things she'd been working on in an attempt to fix her swing problem. She'd adjusted her grip, stance, takeaway, club path, and just about everything else she could think of.

She was hoping I would tell her what was wrong with her swing so she could fix it and get back on track.

There was no doubt her swing wasn't working, but I knew her swing wasn't the problem and talking about swing mechanics would only make things worse. So, I decided to see if I could help her get her swing back by using a different approach.

"When was the last time you had your swing?" I asked.

"Around three months ago," she replied.

"Do you remember a specific round where you last had it?" She nodded yes. "Did you like the swing you had back then?"

Swing Habits Don't Just Disappear

If your golf swing appears to change from one shot to the next, one hole to the next, or one day to the next, it's not your swing that's changing; it's your state of mind.

Changing a swing habit takes time – often three weeks to a year. If you can't change your swing habit in a matter of minutes, you certainly can't "lose" your swing in that time either!

"Yes! Very much," she said emphatically. "I just wish I could have it back again!"

"Well, let's do this," I suggested, somewhat slyly. "Take some swings without a ball and do your best to show me the swing you used to have. That way I can compare your old swing with the swing you have now."

She agreed, and after taking her first practice swing, I asked, "If we call the swing you had three months ago a '10,' on a scale from 1 to 10, how would you rate that last swing?"

"A '2'," she replied, still sounding hopeless.

"Okay. What would have to change in that last swing to make it more like the swing you used to have?"

"It would need to be a lot smoother, and I wouldn't see my club coming way back over my head."

"Great. Why don't you take another practice swing, then rate it again."

She swung again, and I asked, "On a scale from 1 to 10, how would you rate that practice swing in comparison to your '10' swing from before?" We repeated this process over and over again.

If she rated her practice swing less than a "10," I asked her, "What would you need to change to make that swing closer to the swing you used to have?"

As she continued to swing and rate her practice swings in relation to the swing she used to have, something amazing started to happen. By keeping her brain focused on her old swing (the swing she wanted back), her practice swings began moving closer and closer to it.

Her numbers went from 3's and 4's to 7's and 8's. She even started having an occasional "10." The progression wasn't a straight line, but on average, her numbers steadily increased.

> **Keep your "10" swing in mind, and you will see more and more of your best swings.**

Once she made enough "10" practice swings, I knew the swing she wanted was close to the surface. Now, it was just a matter of getting it to show up with a golf ball.

"I have a good picture of the swing you want now, so why don't you hit some golf balls, and I'll compare the swing you have now to the swing you want. Just one thing before you begin," I said, "be sure to make a '10' practice swing before hitting each ball, and then rate every shot, just like you did when you weren't hitting a ball."

Within ten minutes, she was striking the golf ball just like her old self! It was hard to believe this was the same golfer I watched topping and shanking the ball only minutes earlier. You would have thought they were completely different people.

By redirecting her brain to the "10" swing she wanted, her real swing habit was quickly resurrected.

My most difficult task was helping her understand how she could see such a dramatic improvement without ever "changing her swing." It seemed too good to be true!

Miracles Happen

Watching Sammy go from topping and shanking to hitting long, straight, beautiful shots was a miracle. Happily, I've witnessed that same miracle many times since!

Generally speaking, the Miracle Swing Change Process brings your best swing to the surface, and the results are immediate. It works EVERY time ... without fail!

You can use the Miracle Swing Change Process to uncover your real swing habit too – the best swing you have right now.

Three Simple Steps

The Miracle Swing Change Process will help you optimize your swing in many ways. In addition to finding a "lost" swing, it can be used to improve your tempo and balance, make your swing smoother, and remove unnecessary tension.

Focusing on each of these aspects individually leads to the best results. However, the first time you use this process, I recommend starting with one simple goal: to take your practice swing to the ball.

Your practice swing represents your real swing habit much more than your "ball swing," especially if you've never taken the time to optimize your swing before. Specifically, it's smoother, closer to your ideal tempo, and more relaxed, making it a perfect starting point.

Whether your goal is to find a lost swing, bring your practice swing to the ball, or improve your smoothness, tempo, or balance, the three steps are exactly the same:

1. Rehearse a perfect "10"
2. Rate your ball swing
3. Repeat the process

To help you better understand how each step of the process works, I will walk you through another real-life scenario.

Help! My Club Championship is Next Week!

Bill was a very competitive single-digit handicap golfer whose scores had been climbing over the past few months. With his club championship only a week away, he was seriously considering withdrawing from the tournament.

When he met me for his lesson, he was unsure about what to do. He would consider playing if we could somehow get his swing back on track. But, his swing had been so erratic lately, it would take a miracle, and he didn't believe that was possible.

Bill was convinced he was having a swing problem and he wanted my help figuring it out. After listening to everything Bill said he'd been working on, I realized his golf swing was just fine.

(continued from previous page)

He'd been over-thinking every aspect of his swing and testing out different tips for the past month, trying to fix his "problem."

It was clear to me that his problem was conscious interference with his swing. The "vicious cycle" had settled in, eroding his confidence. It was no wonder he had been getting worse and worse!

I explained that one week wasn't enough time to make a swing change, and that I didn't think his swing was the real problem anyway.

"However," I said, "I would be happy to show you a process that will help you get better results from the swing habit you currently own. It's been known to produce dramatic results in a very short time."

Like most golfers, Bill wasn't even sure he had a swing habit anymore. Nonetheless, he decided to give it a try. "I guess it can't hurt," he replied, doubt in his voice.

I explained how and why swing optimization worked. Then I showed him the simple 3-step process.

He called one week later about to burst. "I did it! I did it! I won the club championship! By just thinking about my '10' swing, my other swing thoughts disappeared, my confidence came back, and my swing felt great. Thank you so much! It was unbelievable!"

Jim Realized He Didn't Want a Swing Change

An older gentleman called me for some golf lessons because he wanted to become more consistent. I'll call him Jim.

Jim, a 20-handicap golfer, played two or three times a week with his men's club and with some buddies. Discussing his goals and time availability, I found that he was retired and could practice as much as he wanted.

After talking about his ball flight, swing beliefs, and other factors, he decided he wanted to change his club path. He was losing distance and topping five to six tee shots a round because of an outside-in path. We spent time on his new swing change and off he went.

> # The Miracle Swing Change Process
>
> ### *Step 1*
> Rehearse a perfect "10"
>
> ### *Step 2*
> Rate your ball swing
>
> ### *Step 3*
> Repeat the process

Two weeks later Jim returned for his next lesson, unhappy with his progress. "My scores have gone up, and I've lost confidence since I've been practicing my swing change," he told me.

"Are you thinking about your swing while playing?" I asked.

"Yes," he said. "I'm thinking about my new swing every time I hit the ball, both on the range and on the course."

Immediately, I explained what often happens when golfers have swing thoughts on the course. Then we talked more about the habit change process – the time involved, the potential ups and downs, and so on.

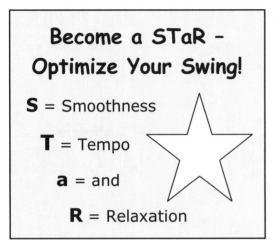

**Become a STaR –
Optimize Your Swing!**

S = Smoothness

T = Tempo

a = and

R = Relaxation

Jim thought it would be impossible to stop thinking about his swing on the course, and he didn't want to continue the swing change if it meant his scores might be affected. So, I recommended that we shift gears and optimize his current swing habit instead.

I discussed how swing optimization and swing change differ, and he was excited about the possibility of seeing his best swings more often and lowering his scores again. "Maybe after I optimize my swing I'll even consider making a swing change again," he said optimistically.

"Sounds great," I said, knowing it would always be an option.

Step 1 – Rehearse a Perfect "10"

"So, here's what we're going to do," I told Jim. "I'm going to show you how to take your practice swing to the ball. It's a very simple process. All you need to do is take some practice swings and rate them. Would you prefer to use a scale from 1 to 5, or 1 to 10?"

After he chose 1 to 10, I continued. "Okay. Take a couple of practice swings to loosen up, and then we'll start rating them. What we're looking for is your best practice swing – a '10' on a scale from 1 to 10."

Jim took a few warm-up swings, then I began the process by asking him, "How would you rate that one?"

"I don't know, maybe a '5'?" he said, not quite sure how the rating process worked.

"Don't worry. There's no right or wrong answer," I assured him. "Just rate your practice swing in comparison to the best practice swing you think you could make right now."

> **To optimize your swing, the first step is to SEE and FEEL exactly what you want.**

"Then that was a '5' or '6'," Jim said, more confidently.

"What would make it closer to a '10'?"

"I don't know. Maybe I could swing a little slower. Let me try again."

Jim took several swings, and I asked him to rate each one. As his numbers increased, and he reached a few "10's," I adjusted my questioning slightly.

"Can you think of anything that could make your practice swing feel even better?" I asked, double-checking that he had found his true "10."

Jim thought about it, and then he took a few more swings until we were both sure that he had his "10."

Taking a break from my story for a minute (as noted by these italics), I want to remind you that Jim had yet to hit any golf balls. In this first step my goal was to help him FEEL exactly what his "10" swing was like.

In my experience, the biggest challenge of this step is to be patient and wait for a "10." You may feel the urge to rush the process so you can hit a ball, figuring that a 7, 8, or 9 is "good enough." It's not.

The more precise you are, the faster your swing will improve. So, make sure you rehearse a true "10" before moving on.

Another challenge at this stage is to trust that you know a "10" when you get one. I've seen golfers reach "9" and stop there, afraid that rating their practice swing as a "10" might somehow mean it can't get any better.

A "10" isn't the best swing you could ever make in your life. Rather, it's the best practice swing you are capable of right now.

Allow five to ten minutes for this step. If it takes longer than that, it means you're TRYING to make a perfect practice swing (i.e., consciously interfering). Instead, just take a regular practice swing and rate how it feels. Keep it simple ... because it is.

Step 2 – Rate Your Ball Swing

"Okay Jim, the next step is to hit a ball. It's a good idea to have the ball teed up and ready to go. Placing it on a tee makes contact easier so you can stay focused on the feel of your swing and not be distracted by the ball. However, you can also play the ball from the ground, if you prefer.

"With the feeling of your '10' swing fresh in your mind, just step up to your ball and swing. After you swing, rate your ball swing on a scale from 1 to 10, just like you rated your practice swing.

"Be sure to rate the FEEL of your swing, and not your contact or the results of your shot. Any questions?"

"Nope," Jim said, shaking his head.

Jim made a "10" practice swing, then stepped up and hit the ball, exactly as we had discussed. "How would you rate that swing?" I asked.

> # Easy as 1, 2, 3!
>
> ### Step 1 - Rehearse a "10"
> SEE and FEEL a "10" practice swing before ever hitting a ball
>
> ### Step 2 - Rate Your Ball Swing
> Rate how your ball swing FEELS
>
> ### Step 3 - Repeat the Process
> Stay FOCUSED on the one change you're making

"It was pretty good, I guess."

Wanting Jim to be more specific, I asked him a different question. "On a scale from 1 to 10, how would you rate that swing in relation to your practice swing?"

"I guess I'd give it a '6'."

"Now, are you rating the results of the shot or how your swing actually felt?" I asked, wanting to make sure he clearly understood the difference.

"I think I might be rating the shot more than the feeling of the swing. Let me try that again."

Step 3 – Repeat the Process

Jim made another "10" practice swing, then stepped up to the ball and hit it. "That was a '7'," he said, confidently.

"I agree," I said, happy to see that we concurred. "So, what would make it more like your practice swing?"

Jim answered and we repeated the process over and over until he was starting to rate more of his ball swings in the "9" and "10" range.

This process works 100% of the time because you repeatedly focus on your "10" swing.

If you noticed, I never asked Jim, "What was wrong with that last swing?" That would have pointed Jim's thinking in the wrong direction. I always asked, "What would make that swing more like your '10'?" The secret of this process is to stay focused on your best swing 100% of the time.

It's also important to stick with the FEEL of your swing. I would never ask you to THINK about your swing mechanics in any way. I would simply ask you to rate your swing and let your body make any necessary adjustments.

When done the way I've described above, the Miracle Swing Change Process is fun, and the results are truly miraculous!

A Happy Ending

Jim showed up one day unexpectedly while I was teaching a lesson, a few weeks after his last session. After waiting patiently, he ran over and gave me a giant hug.

"You won't believe what happened," he exclaimed, beaming from ear to ear. "I'm hitting the ball better than ever. My scores are even lower than when we began! I can't believe it because I'm not thinking about anything! I've just been rating how my swing feels."

Jim's excitement was awesome.

A month later, Jim visited me again with news that his swing was still improving. "This is the only thing I'll ever work on from now on!" he said, proudly.

Jim's story is not unique. Optimizing your swing produces immediate results and helps you shoot lower scores right away. (Unfortunately, the opposite sometimes happens when you're trying to change the mechanics of your swing.)

Swing optimization works so well that many golfers reach their scoring goals and swing goals without ever needing to change their swing mechanics again. Like Jim, once you realize how wonderful your golf swing already is, you too may decide to stick with swing optimization FOREVER!

C'mon, It's Only a Month!

You'll never know how good your swing really is until you optimize it. Take a break from swing change for just one month and make a commitment to use the *Miracle Swing Change Process* instead. One month is all you'll need to experience what a dramatic difference optimizing your golf swing can make!

Chapter 8

Change
is
Good

Can You Feel the Excitement?

If you spend the next month using the Miracle Swing Change Process to optimize your golf swing, the improvement you see will be absolutely amazing. There's a good chance you will never need to focus on anything else ever again. But what if you want to *change* your swing habit?

I've been presenting mental game seminars for men's and women's golf clubs and associations since the mid-1980's. During these seminars, I talk about states of mind, routines, strategy, what to practice, how to practice, and so on. The feedback has always been excellent, with participants telling me that the programs are inspiring, motivating, entertaining, life changing, and fun.

No matter how useful or compelling my mental game information is, though, something changes when I begin talking about swing mechanics. Amazingly, I almost always feel an increase of energy in the room. It's as though some of the participants were thinking, "This mental game stuff is great, but I'm really excited that we get to talk about our golf swings now!"

Of course, I was talking about their golf swings the entire time. However, when I started talking specifically about set-up positions, weight shifts, and backswings, they really lit up.

If that's true for you, here it is ... the chapter you've been waiting for! We're going to shift gears now. Instead of talking about *optimizing* your current swing habit, we're going to focus on *changing* your swing mechanics so you can achieve ultimate consistency, maximum distance, and pinpoint accuracy!

Real Swing Changes Are Awesome

Swing optimization isn't the only process that can lead to miraculous results. Sometimes a change to your grip, stance, takeaway, and so forth, is exactly what you need.

Changing your swing can be fun and extremely rewarding. The secret is to stick with changes that relate directly to impact and to steer clear of changes masquerading as the "right way" to swing.

To Optimize or To Change?
That is the Question

Swing *optimization* and swing *change* will both improve your swing when done properly, but the approach you take with each process is quite different.

Once you understand how each works, you can decide which type of change fits you better based on your personal goals and available practice time.

Here are two helpful guidelines:

- If you don't choose to make the time commitment a swing *change* requires, then *optimize* your current swing habit instead.

- If your "practice swing" already shows up regularly when you hit a golf ball and you know you will stick with a change until completion, then choose to *change* your swing habit.

Real swing changes – those that affect impact – will make your swing better and better. Other swing changes – those you try to make because you believe they're the "right way" to swing – may not tie directly to impact and, therefore, can't guarantee improvement.

A real swing change isn't about making your golf swing *look* good; it's about attaining optimal impact – the moment of truth in your swing.

To *change* your swing habit, you need to understand exactly what must *change* at impact to achieve the results you want. For example, what has to happen between your club and ball to get the ball airborne? To hit a straight shot? To hit the ball farther? And so on.

Swing Change Boils Down to 4 Things

In the past, whenever you've had a swing problem like slicing, hooking, or topping, you may have asked yourself, "What am I doing wrong?" More specifically, "Am I lifting my head?" "Is my front arm straight?" Or, "Am I standing too far from the ball?" could easily have entered your mind.

With the I-Swing System, it's not, "What am *I* doing wrong?" The question is, "What needs to happen at impact to get the results I want?" Or, said differently, "What is wrong with my *club position* at impact?"

When you ask yourself, "What am I doing wrong?" you become vulnerable to a barrage of *subjective* swing ideas about how you should move your body. When you ask, "What is wrong with my club position at impact?" you take an entirely different approach, one that leads to an *objective* answer about your club.

Focusing directly on your club position at impact is the most effective way to *change* your swing habit. It's also faster and easier because there are only four things that need to happen to get the results you want.

These are the conditions that need to be true at impact to hit a solid, straight, airborne shot on target:

1. **CONTACT** – The sweet spot of your club must connect with your golf ball

2. **DIRECTION** – Your clubface and path must be square to your target line

3. **DISTANCE** – Your club must be moving at the appropriate speed

4. **TRAJECTORY** – Your club must have the desired loft

"Body Mechanics" vs. "Club Mechanics"

Body mechanics ...
are the mechanics of your body – (e.g., the vast number of positions and motions of your head, shoulders, arms, hands, torso, hips, knees, feet, etc.)

Club mechanics ...
are the mechanics of your club – (e.g., clubface, path, loft, speed, etc.)

To get your club into the proper position at impact, your best bet is to focus on the few "works every time" club mechanics, rather than the unlimited number of "might work" body mechanics.

These same four swing characteristics are the keys to eliminating slices, adding distance to your tee shots, and improving your short game. Whether you are a new golfer, intermediate golfer, advanced golfer, recreational golfer, tournament player, or touring pro, these four apply exactly the same.

What Change Do You Want to Make?

First and foremost, to *change* your swing habit, you need to change one of the four aspects of impact – contact, direction, distance or trajectory. In the next four chapters, I will show you everything you need to know about each.

Your golf swing will no longer be a mystery. You'll never have to ask, "What did I do wrong?" You will learn what causes topped shots, sliced shots, and every other kind of miss-hit. More importantly, you will know exactly what must happen at impact to achieve any swing goal you could ever want.

Swing changes take time. But, if you have the time, are ready to make the commitment, and you know the right change to make, a swing change can make a huge difference in your game.

Want to Make a Swing Change?

Then, you need to change one of these "Fab Four" –

- *Contact*
- *Direction*
- *Distance*
- *Trajectory*

Chapter 9

No More Mystery!

The Most Important Aspect of Impact

CONTACT, when the surface of your clubhead meets the ball, is the most important aspect of impact because it affects all three of the other aspects as well – direction, distance, and trajectory.

> # Too Many ...
>
> ### Grounders?
>
> ### Pop-Ups?
>
> ### Miss-Hits?
>
> ### Shanks?
>
> ### Better CONTACT
> ### is your solution.

For example, when you strike the ball with the toe of your club, the shot is likely to stray off the intended line, travel shorter than expected, and have a different trajectory than desired.

Like all aspects of impact, contact is not mysterious. It is based solely on how the head of your golf club and golf ball connect.

There are several terms used to describe meetings of the clubhead and ball that have not gone according to plan: thin shots, fat shots, topped shots, bladed shots, skulled shots, shanks, chunks, chilly dips, and so on.

Fortunately, there are very simple and specific reasons why these miss-hits happen.

Take the Mystery Out of Your Shots

Your golf ball goes where it goes for very specific reasons. It's not about how the stars are aligned or the position of your head. It's about the forces that are applied to the ball by your golf club at impact.

I'm told it's basic physics. Not being a physicist, I'm not really even sure what "basic physics" means, but I do know that your golf ball flies or doesn't fly based on how your golf club connects with it.

My goal is for you to understand exactly what happens at impact between your club and ball that causes your ball to go where it goes. With that knowledge, you can eliminate the anxiety and mini-panic attacks triggered by miss-hits, and avoid falling into the "vicious cycle" of fixing your swing. You can enjoy the peaceful, calm confidence that comes from knowing exactly what DID happen at impact.

Impact is Your Friend

If you're like most golfers, the truth is you know very little about impact. You've probably been told over and over again that you should keep your head down and your front arm straight, but there's a good chance you've never been told about the *true* fundamentals of your golf swing.

When I ask golfers if they know what causes a topped shot, they often hesitate, waiver, and guess something related to their bodies. Typical responses might be: "I think I top shots because I lift my head." "Is it because I'm raising my body?" And, "I guess I need to learn how to stay down longer."

Isn't it amazing that something so important is so rarely discussed?

**Guarantee results
by learning about impact
and achieving solid contact.**

Impact is the single most important aspect of your swing, yet most of the attention given to improvement is lavished on swing methods. It's like trying to learn how to hit a baseball by focusing on everything EXCEPT the bat and ball.

Well, don't let the lack of attention to the "club-ball encounter" fool you. If you want to change your swing, the key is to thoroughly understand impact.

Even if you are one of those rare individuals who already knows a great deal about impact, I still recommend reading the next few chapters. There's nothing more important to reinforce, and you may even pick up some important distinctions.

With that in mind, grab a club if you have one handy. It's time to dive in again!

Meeting at the Sweet Spot

To achieve solid contact, the sweet spot of the golf club (photo 9-1) needs to meet with the golf ball.

9-1

The "sweet spot"

The size of the sweet spot varies with club design, but generally speaking, it's an elliptical area centered in the lower part of the clubface.

To make sure your golf ball meets with the sweet spot of your club, there are two important things to understand:

1. Your club *shaft* must be tilted toward your target to ensure the leading edge of your club is below the ball (photo 9-2).

2. Your club must swing low enough for the leading edge of your clubhead to stay below the ball (i.e., if your golf ball is resting on the ground, the leading edge of your clubhead must brush the earth as you swing).

9-2

Club shaft is tilted toward the target

The "leading edge" is the front edge of the bottom of your club (photo 9-3).

9-3

The "leading edge"

Notice how the leading edge of the club is below the golf ball in photo 9-4 below, allowing the sweet spot of the club to meet solidly with the ball.

9-4

The "leading edge" is below the ball

If you pick up your golf club and look closely at the head (which I highly recommend doing as you read this), you will see how the leading edge stays down when the club shaft is tilted toward the target (photo 9-5), and moves up as the club shaft tilts back (photo 9-6).

9-5

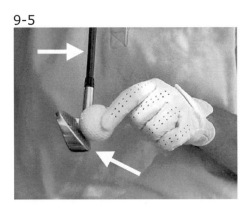

The "leading edge" stays down when the club shaft is tilted toward the target

9-6

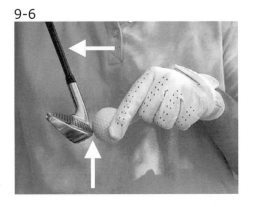

The "leading edge" moves up as the club shaft tilts back

Club Shaft Tilt is Extremely Important

If your club shaft is tilted away from your target, the leading edge of your club will lift up and contact the ball instead of the sweet spot, causing topped, skulled or bladed shots (photo 9-6 on previous page and 9-7 below).

9-7

Tilting the club shaft away from the target causes the leading edge of the club to lift up

The primary cause of this improper club shaft tilt is the "breaking down" of the front wrist, often referred to as "early release," "flipping," or "scooping."

In an effort to solve this problem, many golfers try to "lift" the ball into the air by "flipping" their wrists even more. Of course, this just lifts the leading edge of the club higher, making solid contact even less likely.

So, remember to keep the leading edge of your club beneath the ball at impact by making sure your club shaft is tilted toward your target. You'll get solid contact more often, resulting in more good shots and fewer bad shots (photo 9-8).

9-8

The leading edge of the club is below the ball

The Exception to the Rule

Normally, the only way to achieve solid contact is to keep your club shaft tilted toward the target so the leading edge of your club stays below the ball.

However, there is one instance when it is possible to contact the ball with the sweet spot of your club AND have the club shaft tilted back at the same time – namely, when the ball lies in fluffy grass.

For example, a fluffy lie leaves room for the leading edge of your club to lift up AND stay below the ball at the same time (photo 9-9). Advanced players could use this technique to produce a higher, more lofted, "lob" shot.

9-9

In a fluffy lie, the leading edge
of the club can be below the ball
even with the club shaft tilted back

Two Ways to Top a Ball

Is that the craziest heading you've ever read in a golf swing book? Why would you ever want to learn how to top a ball? Easy ... to learn more about contact.

There are two distinctly different ways to top a golf ball – a "lift top" and a "flip top." While the results are the same, your club position for each is quite different. Therefore, the way to correct these miss-hits differs, too.

A "lift top" occurs when the entire club is lifted, even though your club shaft may be tilted properly (photo 9-10).

9-10

A "lift" top – the entire golf club lifts

A "flip top" occurs when your club shaft is tilted back, even though your club itself may not be lifted (photo 9-11).

9-11

A "flip" top – the club shaft tilts back

If you tend to "lift top" the ball, you don't actually need a swing change. You just need to swing your club lower so the leading edge brushes the ground as you swing.

If you tend to "flip top" the ball, a swing change will be necessary to correct the habit of "flipping" your wrists through impact.

A swing change in this case will involve learning what it's like to swing with your club shaft tilted toward your target at impact. This is also commonly referred to as, "keeping your hands in front of the ball," "leading with your hands," or "leading with the club handle."

"These Golf Professionals Can't Hit Worth a Darn!"

As an LPGA Teaching Professional, I earn points each year to maintain my certification. The system is similar to the continuing education requirements for nurses and other professionals.

It was high season in the Palm Springs area, and we had about 25 LPGA Teaching Professionals gathered for a workshop at a busy private country club. Our main focus was the detection and correction of common ball flight problems.

We talked about ball flight principles all morning. Then, we took what we had learned to the driving range with the objective of experiencing the ball flight problems for ourselves.

Word had spread that a group of LPGA Professionals was on site, so there were quite a few members gathered behind the range to watch us.

As we were practicing hitting grounders, shanks, slices, and hooks, I happened to glance over at the members. The looks on their faces were priceless. The crowd obviously had no idea that our goal was to hit those shots on purpose!

No Need to Flip Over This!

It's the contact with your clubface that causes the ball to fly into the air, and not the flipping of your wrists.

Keep the leading edge of your clubhead below the ball, or the only result you will "physics-ally" see is a topped shot!

Can You Shank a Ball on Purpose?

Some golfers consider "the shanks" one of the most dreaded problems in golf. They fear being stuck in a nightmare groove, endlessly shanking the ball. Even when their contact is fine, these golfers don't want to hear the "s" word, afraid that the thought alone will bring on the shanks.

Ever since attending the LPGA seminar in Palm Springs where all the participants practiced topping and shanking shots, one of my favorite ways to "wow" a crowd is to shank a ball on purpose.

It's even more fun when I hit a great shot right after it, proving that one shank doesn't have to lead to another!

Like every shot in golf, a shank is not a mystery. The name itself gives it away. A shank occurs when the "shank" of your golf club (a.k.a., the "hosel") contacts your golf ball. Because the hosel is round, connecting with it causes the ball to travel offline and usually shorter than intended (photo 9-12).

9-12

The "shank" of the club contacting the ball

If you really want to have some fun, teach yourself to purposely shank a shot. Your new found expertise could bring great entertainment value to your family and friends. More importantly, when you learn how to shank a shot on purpose, you will also know how to prevent one from sneaking into your repertoire!

It's No Mystery!

If you top or shank a shot, you may wonder what you did to cause it, but one thing should never be a mystery … where the clubhead met the ball.

If you want solid contact, keep your club shaft tilted toward the target so the leading edge of your clubface stays below the ball. There's no mystery about it!

Chapter 10

Your Path,
Your Choice

How Do You Want Your Ball to Fly?

The first step to controlling how your golf ball flies is to make solid contact, as described in Chapter 9. Assuming that you have solid contact, this chapter will help you understand the nine possible ball flight patterns, so you can control the direction of your shots.

> # Too Many ...
>
> Slices?
>
> Hooks?
>
> Pulls?
>
> Pushes?
>
> Better DIRECTION
> is your solution.

Do you have a slice that requires aiming two fairways over? Do you have a wicked hook? Do you pull or push too many shots?

Do you prefer your golf ball to fly straight at your target, to draw a little so you can get some extra distance, or to fade a bit so it lands more softly on the greens?

If you'd like to know how to hit a straight shot, a draw, or a fade, it's time to understand and integrate DIRECTION into your performance. By the end of this chapter, you will know exactly what causes your golf ball to fly straight, to the left, to the right, and curve in either direction.

Straight at Your Target

If your goal is to hit a straight shot, the path of the clubhead and the leading edge of the clubface must be square to the target line at impact (photo 10-1).

The "target line" is an imaginary line that extends through and beyond your ball and target (illustration 10-2).

10-1

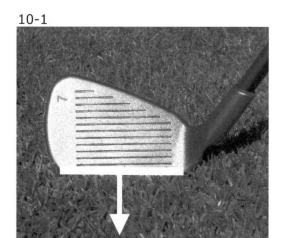

"Square" clubface and path

10-2

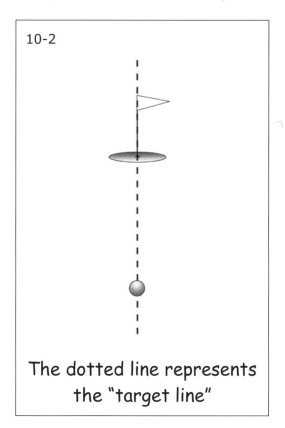

The dotted line represents
the "target line"

There are three basic clubface positions – open, closed, and square. For a right-handed golfer, the "open" clubface is aimed to the right of the target (photo 10-3), the "closed" clubface is aimed to the left of the target (photo 10-4), and the "square" clubface is aimed directly at the target (photo 10-5).

10-3

10-4

"Open" clubface   "Closed" clubface

10-5

"Square" clubface

In photo 10-5 on the previous page, does the clubface look like it's facing to the right? If so, take a closer look.

The *top* of the clubface is facing to the right, but the *bottom* of the clubface is square, or perpendicular, to the target line.

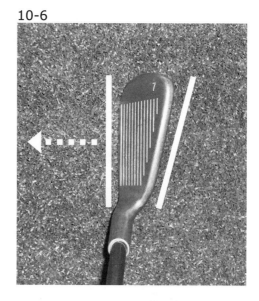

10-6

Every iron I've ever seen is designed with the top of the clubhead set at an angle relative to the bottom (photo 10-6). This can create the optical illusion that the clubface is open, when in reality, it's square.

The leading edge is square to the target line

Don't let the top of the club fool you. If you square the TOP of your clubhead to your target line, thinking you are squaring the clubface, you will really be setting up with the clubface in a closed position.

So, be sure to focus on the leading edge of the clubface when lining up your shots (photo 10-6).

Case Closed

Your clubface is "closed" when the TOP of the clubhead is square to the target line, and "square" when the BOTTOM of the clubhead is square to the target line.

Which Path Do You Choose?

In addition to the three basic clubface positions, there are also three basic clubhead paths – left, straight, and right (illustration 10-7).

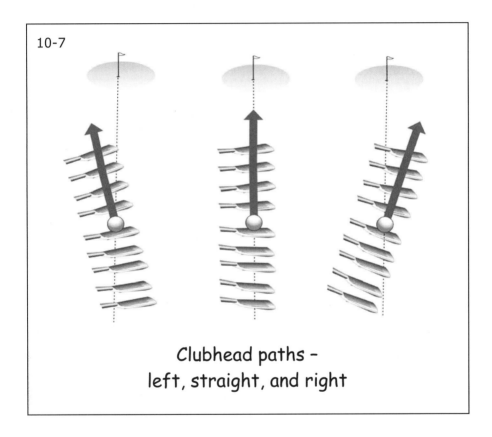

10-7

Clubhead paths –
left, straight, and right

Generally speaking, if you swing your clubhead on a path to the left, your golf ball will take off to the left. If you swing on a path square to your target, your golf ball will take off straight at your target. If you swing on a path to the right, your golf ball will take off to the right, as demonstrated by the illustration above.

Fly Baby, Fly!

After the initial take off, your ball will either keep flying straight along your initial path, or it will curve to the left or right of your initial path (illustration 10-8). How it flies is based on the position of the clubface in relation to the clubhead path.

If you're right-handed and your clubface is closed to your path, the ball will curve left. If it's square to your path, it will fly straight. And, if it's open to your path, the ball will curve right. If you're left-handed, the exact opposite is true.

Earlier, I wrote that the curve of your shot is based on your clubface position "in relation to the *clubhead path.*" Notice that I didn't write "in relation to the *target line.*" This is an important distinction.

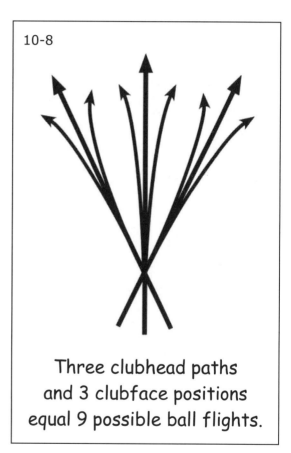

10-8

Three clubhead paths and 3 clubface positions equal 9 possible ball flights.

The clubhead path is defined in relation to the target line (left, straight, right). However, the clubface position is defined in relation to the clubhead path (open, square, closed). The nine possible ball flights represent the "combined" effects of the clubhead path and clubface.

Da Plane, Da Plane

The swing plane, often misunderstood, is another important aspect of DIRECTION. A golf club is designed with the shaft set at an angle to the clubhead – commonly referred to as the "lie angle." So when you swing, the path of your club will follow a similar angle. A common misconception is that the clubhead must be swung along the target line.

10-9

An "inclined" swing plane

For your clubhead path to be straight through impact, your club needs to swing on an inclined plane (photo 10-9). If your image of a swing plane is vertical, like a Ferris wheel, you need to adjust your image!

Because the club swings on an inclined plane, if you were to view the path of the clubhead from above, you would see that it travels on an arc, inside the target line on the backswing, back to the target line at impact, and then inside the target line again after impact (illustration 10-10).

The term "inside," used in the paragraph above, refers to the side of the target line that the golfer stands on.

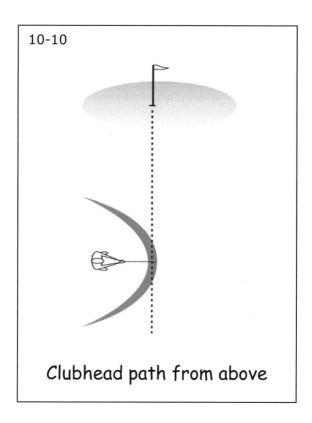

Clubhead path from above

July 4th Sparklers Light the Way!

If you've ever celebrated July 4th with sparklers, you know they leave a really cool trail of light when you wave them through the air. As a kid, I remember using sparklers to draw my name and other things in the sky.

If you pretend that the head of your golf club is a sparkler, and you imagine it leaving a trail of light as you swing, that trail of light would be your clubhead path.

That's Great! Now What Do I Do?

Once you *understand* what causes your golf ball to fly in different directions, it's time for you to *experience* the different swings. That's where your real learning happens. The most effective and fun way to do that is to hit shots that demonstrate all nine ball flight patterns:

1. Straight left
2. Left with a curve left
3. Left with a curve right
4. Straight
5. Straight with a curve left
6. Straight with a curve right
7. Straight right
8. Right with a curve left
9. Right with a curve right

Here's how:

1st - Pick the ball flight pattern you want to create.

2nd - Remind yourself which clubhead path and clubface position is required at impact for that particular ball flight (e.g., to hit a shot "straight left," your clubhead path must swing to the left, and your clubface must be square to that *path*).

3rd – See if you can create that ball flight pattern.
(Note: This exercise is usually best accomplished using a 5 or 6 iron because of their length and loft.)

Look at the two charts on the next page (one is for right-handed golfers and the other is for left-handed golfers). Study your chart. If you're not 100% sure which club path and clubface position causes each particular ball flight pattern, I recommend making a copy of the chart and carrying it with you to the range.

For a RIGHT-Handed Golfer

Ball Flight	Clubhead Path	Clubface (in relation to path)
Straight left	Left	Square
Left with a curve left	Left	Closed
Left with a curve right	Left	Open
Straight	Straight	Square
Straight with a curve left	Straight	Closed
Straight with a curve right	Straight	Open
Straight right	Right	Square
Right with a curve left	Right	Closed
Right with a curve right	Right	Open

For a LEFT-Handed Golfer

Ball Flight	Clubhead Path	Clubface (in relation to path)
Straight left	Left	Square
Left with a curve left	Left	Open
Left with a curve right	Left	Closed
Straight	Straight	Square
Straight with a curve left	Straight	Open
Straight with a curve right	Straight	Closed
Straight right	Right	Square
Right with a curve left	Right	Open
Right with a curve right	Right	Closed

You can also use the information in the chart to understand what happens at impact when you hit an unwanted shot. For example, if you're a right-handed golfer and you hit a "slice" that starts along the target line and then curves to the right, you will know it was caused by a square club path and open clubface (see the example on the left of illustration 10-11 below).

If you hit a shot that starts to the left of the target line and then curves right, you will know that your club path was to the left (commonly referred to as an "outside-in" club path), and your clubface was open to the path (see the example on the right of illustration 10-11 below).

Remember, your golf ball never lies! It always tells the truth about what happens at impact.

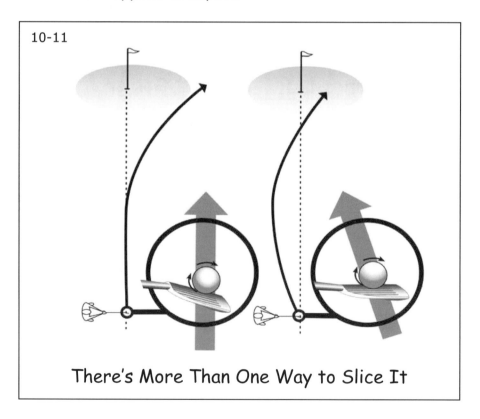

10-11

There's More Than One Way to Slice It

It might also help you to realize that slicing a ball in golf is similar to curving a tennis ball, ping pong ball, or soccer ball (illustration 10-12).

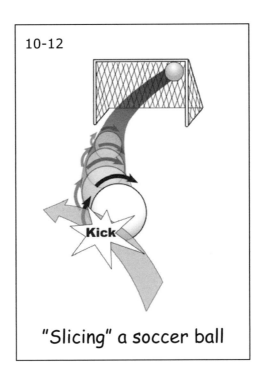

10-12

"Slicing" a soccer ball

Choose Your Direction

Bottom line, if you want to hit a straight shot toward a target, make sure your clubhead path and clubface are square to your target line at impact. If, instead, your clubhead path is to the left or right, or your clubface position is open or closed, start looking for your ball because it won't be at your target!

When a golf shot flies offline, one thing should never be a mystery – the clubhead path and clubface position at impact.

Chapter 11

Longer, Farther, Faster

How Far Do You Want to Go?

Contact and direction are great, but if you're like most golfers, you want DISTANCE! Given solid contact, that means you need more CLUBHEAD SPEED.

Whether you want to hit the ball farther, regain some distance you've lost, or control the distance of your short game shots better, this chapter is for you.

Are You ...

Hitting Short?

Hitting Long?

Losing Power?

DISTANCE control is your solution.

With the possible exception of excessive spin, the slower your clubhead speed through impact, the shorter your ball will go. The faster your clubhead speed, the farther it will go.

Therefore, if you want to hit your ball a *shorter* distance, you need to *decrease* your clubhead speed. If you want to hit your ball *farther*, you need to *increase* your clubhead speed.

Of course, these statements are only accurate assuming that you are working with a single club and that you make solid contact with each shot – which I will assume throughout this chapter.

You Already Have a Feel for Distance

Ever since you were a kid, you've tossed things – bean bags into clown's mouths, balls into mitts, wads of paper into trash cans, bags of stuff into cars, and the list goes on.

(continued from previous page)

During that time, you developed a feel for distance. Even if you're a new golfer and you've never played another sport in your life, you've done things outside of sports that have given you a feel for distance.

I know this because one of the first things I ask golfers to do when they want to improve their short games is toss golf balls to different targets.

I recommend you do the same. Choose three targets - close, medium, and long range (all distances you can comfortably reach with an underhand toss). Then, toss golf balls to those targets.

As you're tossing, you may notice three things:

1. You already know how to toss the ball different distances without having to think about it.

2. Your arm *automatically* swings back farther when you want to toss the ball farther.

3. No matter how far back your arm swings, it always swings *forward farther* than it swings back.

To apply this same feel for distance to your short game, *pretend* you are tossing your CLUBHEAD to a target. This will give you the FEEL of the swing you need for the shot. Then, hit a ball using that same motion and see how close you get.

Two Main Ways to Control Distance

To control your distance around the greens (i.e., putting, chipping, pitching, and sand shots), it is essential to control the speed of your clubhead through impact. There are two main ways to do this:

1. Speed of your swing
2. Length of your swing

For example, you could swing at a slow, medium, or fast speed. Or, you could make a ¼-length, ½-length, or ¾-length swing. Normally, the "length of your swing" refers to the length of your backswing. It also presumes that your follow through is longer than your backswing.

Most golf professionals teach that the best way to control the distance of your short game shots is to vary the length of your backswing. That's the way most golfers prefer to do it, as well.

At the same time, as an up-and-coming amateur golfer I had the honor of spending two days with a highly respected short game coach who taught me that the best way to change the length of my pitch shots was to vary my clubhead speed. He believed it was better to make a full length swing whenever possible – even for pitch and sand shots – because anything less than a full swing caused timing and tension problems.

I'm not sure which way will work best for you. But, I do know that swing speed and the length of your swing both affect your clubhead speed at impact.

As a rule, shorter, slower swings generate less clubhead speed at impact, resulting in shorter shots. Conversely, longer, faster swings generate greater clubhead speed at impact, resulting in longer shots.

Olympic Ski Jumpers Know - the Farther Back You Go, the More Speed You Get

If you've ever watched Winter Olympic ski jumping, you've seen an image of how backswing length can affect clubhead speed at impact.

Picture a ski jumper getting ready to make a long jump. He steps out onto the steep ramp, crouches down over his skis as aerodynamically as possible, and lets gravity take its course, gaining speed as he goes. All things being equal, the faster he's going at take-off, the longer his jump will be.

If there are two different starting points on the ramp, the farther up the ramp the ski jumper starts, the more speed he will have at take-off. For example, a skier starting at the top of the ramp will have more speed than a skier starting halfway down the ramp, and will therefore travel farther.

You can use this image of a ski jumper to picture how different backswing lengths can affect the distance of your short game shots. For example, the longer your backswing (i.e., the farther up the ramp you start), the more clubhead speed you will have at impact (i.e., take-off), and the farther your golf ball will fly.

The Simplest Way to Increase Your Distance

Clearly, your clubhead speed at impact determines the distance of your shot (illustration 11-1). So, if you want more distance, how do you begin to increase the speed of your swing?

Trying to simply swing faster can be very counter-productive. In doing that, most golfers inadvertently swing "harder" instead of "faster," which causes their muscles to tighten, actually decreasing clubhead speed. Swinging too fast can also throw off your timing, tempo, and balance.

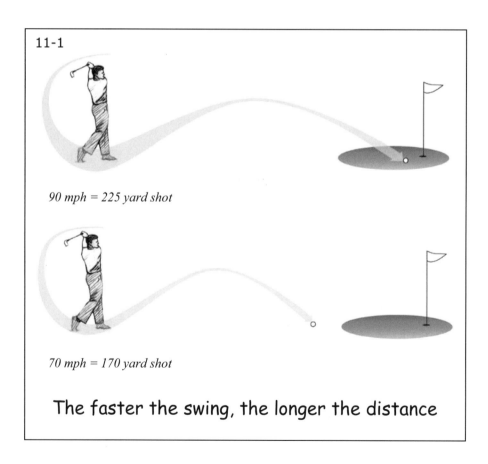

11-1

90 mph = 225 yard shot

70 mph = 170 yard shot

The faster the swing, the longer the distance

Here's what I recommend instead. It's called "release." If you want to add distance to your shots, your release is an important concept to understand.

First, let me tell you my definition of release in case you use the term differently. During the backswing, most golfers cock their wrists, forming an angle between their front arm and club. To me, "release" is the act of straightening that angle in the forward swing.

The release of this angle increases the speed at the end of your club, similar to how the person on the end in a game of "Crack the Whip" travels much faster than the person in the center. Because of this tremendous increase in power, I've fittingly named this the "power angle" (photo 11-2).

11-2

The "Power Angle"

For the "release" to give you maximum clubhead speed at impact:

1. You must form a "power angle" in your backswing.
2. You must release the "power angle" through impact.

If the power angle is released before impact, the power will be released to the air and not the ball. This is commonly referred to as an "early release" (illustration 11-3).

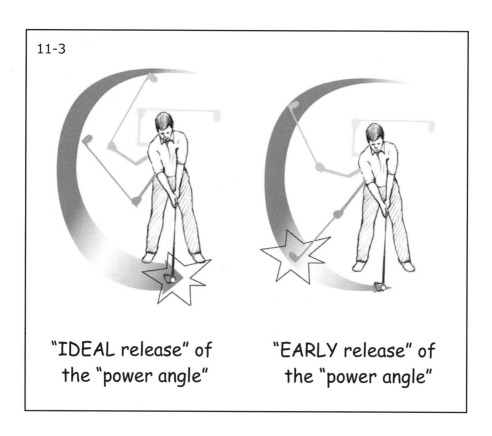

11-3

"IDEAL release" of the "power angle"

"EARLY release" of the "power angle"

On the next two pages, you will see two swing sequences. The top sequence demonstrates an *early release*. You can see how the power angle starts to straighten at the beginning of the forward swing and is already released well before impact.

The bottom sequence demonstrates an *ideal release*. You can see how the power angle is intact during the forward swing, only releasing through impact.

Baseball and Softball Players Know How to Release

Hitting a baseball (or softball) and hitting a golf ball are essentially the same when it comes to release. Pretend you're about to hit a pitch and you'll understand what I mean.

As you stand in the batter's box awaiting the pitch, you've already formed a power angle between your front arm and the bat. As you begin swinging, the power angle stays intact until right before impact, when it finally releases and you smack the ball out of the park.

The most important thing to notice is how the power angle remains at approximately 90-degrees until just before impact. It doesn't start to straighten until it's time for maximum power.

If you want to feel how ineffective an early release is, try it for yourself. Grab a bat, purposely straighten out your power angle early, and notice how strange it feels.

11-4

11-5

At the start of the forward swing, the power angle is starting to release. Compare this with the photo below.

Midway into the forward swing, the power angle has released even more. Compare this with the photo below.

11-8

11-9

At the start of the forward swing, the power angle is still intact. Notice the club and arm form a 90-degree angle.

Midway into the forward swing, the power angle is still intact. Notice that the 90-degree angle is maintained.

11-6

The power angle is almost fully released here. Notice how the front arm and club nearly form a straight line.

11-7

At impact, she was unable to produce maximum clubhead speed because the timing of her release was early.

11-10

Well into the forward swing, the power angle is still nearly 90-degrees, and is just starting to release in preparation for impact.

11-11

At impact, he produced maximum clubhead speed for the shot because the timing of his release was ideal.

How Effective is Your Release?

To determine the effectiveness of your release, there are two things you can check:

1. **Are you making a power angle in your backswing?** If you are forming little or no angle in your backswing, you'll have little or no power to "release" through the ball.

2. **How are you releasing your power angle?** If you are straightening your power angle well before impact, you'll have little or no power to "release" through the ball.

If you discover your release could use some improvement, I'm NOT recommending that you go out and try to change it right away. Before starting any swing change, it's important to create a "Personalized Improvement Plan" that takes your "whole game" into account, prioritizing all the changes you'd like to make.

After the next chapter, I'll show you the best way to apply everything we've covered. For now, just remember this ... if you want to hit the ball farther, you need to increase your clubhead SPEED at impact. There's no mystery about it!

Chapter 12

Low or High,
Let it Fly

How High Do You Want to Fly?

TRAJECTORY is the fourth and final aspect of impact. The first three aspects we covered – contact, direction, and distance – usually get the majority of the attention, but TRAJECTORY is the most important when it comes to controlling the height of your shots.

Do You ...

Hit Shots Too High?

Hit Shots Too Low?

Need a Punch Shot?

TRAJECTORY control

is your solution.

The trajectory of your shot is based on the LOFT of your clubface at impact. (This assumes that all other factors shot to shot are equal.)

Every golf club is designed with a specific amount of loft. For example, the average sand wedge has 55 degrees of loft, the average 7-iron has 35 degrees of loft, and the average 5-iron has 27 degrees of loft (photo 12-1).

12-1

The "loft" of each clubface varies

Since loft is not standardized throughout the golf industry, you can expect some variation between manufacturers (e.g., the standard loft for a 7-iron might be 34-degrees for one company and 36-degrees for another).

In addition, the loft of irons as a whole has decreased over the years due to club companies competing for the right to boast, "Our clubs are the longest hitting clubs ever made!"

While club loft may vary, there is one thing that will always stay the same – to control the height of shots, you need to control the LOFT of your clubhead at impact. If you want to hit the ball higher, you must *increase* loft. If you want to hit lower, you must *decrease* loft.

Obviously, the easiest way to change loft is to change clubs – use a 5-iron instead of a 7-iron if you want to hit lower, or a 9-iron instead of a 7-iron to hit higher. But, there are other ways to change loft, as well. To help you more fully understand loft, I will focus on how to change TRAJECTORY *without* changing clubs.

Got Custom-Fit Clubs?

The golf equipment you use can definitely affect the trajectory of your shots, as well as the other aspects of impact. For example, if your club shafts are too stiff, you will tend to hit the ball lower and shorter than you would with shafts that fit you.

Before deciding on a swing change, contact your local golf professional or certified club-fitter to make sure your equipment – like your golf swing – is CUSTOM-FIT to YOUR BODY!

Three Ways to Change a Club's Loft

Even though a club may be designed with a specific amount of loft, it doesn't mean that same amount of loft will be there at impact. There are several ways you can change the loft of a club *before* and *during* your swing.

For the purposes of this chapter, I'll refer to the built-in loft of a club as its "true loft," and the loft of the club at impact as the "contact loft."

To change the contact loft of a club, there are three things you can change:

1. Ball position
2. Clubface position
3. Club shaft tilt

To DECREASE the contact loft of your club:

1. **Ball Position** – Move the ball *back* in your stance.
2. **Clubface Position** – *Close* the clubface.
3. **Club Shaft Tilt** – Tilt the shaft *toward* the target.

To INCREASE the contact loft of your club:

1. **Ball Position** – Move the ball *forward* in your stance.
2. **Clubface Position** – *Open* the clubface.
3. **Club Shaft Tilt** – Tilt the shaft *away* from the target.

The photos on the next three pages demonstrate loft increase and decrease using a 7-iron. The effects would be similar using any club.

Change Your Ball Position to Change Loft

To DECREASE loft, move your ball/club BACK in your stance. (A lower ball flight usually means more roll upon landing.)

This picture shows "true loft" with a 7-iron.

To INCREASE loft, move your ball/club FORWARD in your stance. Make sure the leading edge of your club stays below the ball.

Open or Close Your Clubface to Change Loft

12-5

To DECREASE loft, CLOSE your clubface. Remember, this will also affect the direction of your shot.

12-6

This picture shows "true loft" with a 7-iron.

12-7

To INCREASE loft, OPEN your clubface. Remember, this will also affect the direction of your shot.

Tilt Your Club Shaft to Change Loft

12-8

To DECREASE loft, tilt your club shaft TOWARD the target.

12-9

This picture shows "true loft" with a 7-iron.

12-10

To INCREASE loft, tilt your club shaft AWAY from the target. Remember, the leading edge must always stay lower than the ball.

The Choice is Yours

Now you know three different ways to increase and decrease the loft of your clubs in order to vary the height of your shots. You can use this information to hit high shots, low shots, and every shot height in-between.

But, why did you need to learn how to change the loft of a club when you can just change clubs? There are several great reasons:

- To give you more shot choices for your full swing
- To give you more shot choices in your short game
- To help you trouble-shoot a swing problem

For example:

- If your ball is under a tree and you need to hit a low, punch shot, but you don't have enough room to swing a longer, less-lofted club, you will know to choose a shorter length club and decrease the loft using one of the three ways we discussed.

- If the rough requires you to play the ball back in your stance in order to get solid contact (decreasing loft), but you also need enough height on the shot to land softly over a bunker, you could choose to play a sand wedge with an open clubface (increasing loft).

- If you're unhappy with low trajectory shots, you can check your ball position, clubface position, and club shaft tilt to determine which one needs to be adjusted.

Experience This For Yourself

The information we've just covered on CONTACT, DIRECTION, DISTANCE, and TRAJECTORY can be used to solve any ball flight problem you may have.

For instance, if you top a ball, you will know that the leading edge of your clubhead is connecting with the middle or upper part of your golf ball. Likewise, if you slice a ball, you will know that your clubface is open to your clubhead path at impact.

Understanding clubhead position at impact is the first step. The next step is to apply this information until it becomes second nature.

But Can You Do It "On Purpose?"

The easiest and most fun way to make the four aspects of impact second nature is to teach yourself how to hit many different types of shots.

For example, go to a driving range and:

- Challenge yourself to top or shank the ball.

- See how much curve you can get on a hook or slice.

- Experiment with different length backswings and notice how shorter and longer swings affect the distance of your short game shots.

- Hit the ball high and low using all three ways we covered in this chapter.

The Mystery is Over!

Recapping Chapters 9 through 12:

To achieve solid CONTACT, the sweet spot of your golf club and golf ball must meet.

To improve your DIRECTION and hit more straight shots, the path of your clubhead and the leading edge of your clubface must be square to the target line at impact.

To increase your DISTANCE, you must increase your clubhead speed at impact.

And last, but certainly not least, to control the TRAJECTORY of your shots, you need to produce the appropriate amount of loft at impact.

By understanding what needs to happen between your clubhead and ball to create all the shots in golf – those you want and those you don't want – your golf swing will absolutely never be a mystery again!

This is BIG!

Every ball flight problem can be solved using the four aspects of impact – CONTACT, DIRECTION, DISTANCE, and TRAJECTORY.

Chapter 13

One
Step at a
Time

Now for the Really Good Stuff

CONGRATULATIONS! You've now learned how to optimize your current swing habit, and what to change between your clubface and ball at impact to solve any swing problem you may have.

It's time to move into the most important part of this book – how to take the information we've covered and apply it to your game so you can have the results you want in the fastest, easiest way possible.

I said it on the very first page and I'm going to say it again, "Golf improvement is only difficult when you're trying to learn the hard way."

If you spend your time working on the *wrong things* and practicing the *wrong way,* golf improvement is difficult. If you focus on the *right things* and practice the *right way,* golf improvement is much easier!

In this chapter, I'll show you how to determine the *right thing* to practice. It is the "WHAT" aspect of your Personalized Improvement Plan (page 50).

The Fastest Way from Here to There

Golf improvement at its simplest is about moving your game from where it is now to where you want it to be, in the shortest, most direct way possible (illustration 13-1).

The most effective way to reach your destination is one step at a time. To ensure your complete success, each step must be SPECIFIC and MEASURABLE. That way you will know exactly what you're changing, you'll be able to track your progress, and you will know when you've arrived. Best of all, you'll know when it's time to CELEBRATE!

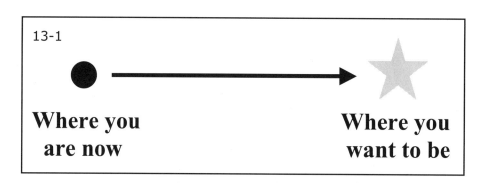

13-1

**Where you
are now**

**Where you
want to be**

For example, when considering a swing change, first choose the aspect of impact that you want to change. Then, choose the precise change you intend to make – the more precise, the better.

One way to check if you are being specific enough is to make sure you can clearly define the contrast between your old way and your new way. For example:

Old way – thinking about your *swing* when you play
New Way – thinking about your *target* when you play

Old way – making a *jerky, rushed "4"* swing
New Way – making a *super smooth "10"* swing

Old way – tilting your club shaft *away* from your target
New way – tilting your club shaft *toward* your target

Old way – swinging your club on a *vertical* swing plane
New way – swinging your club on an *inclined* swing plane

Old way – creating *no angle* in your backswing
New way – creating a *"power angle"* in your backswing

An even better way to guarantee that you are being specific enough is to actually *demonstrate* the EXACT change you plan to make.

My Pet Project

I've always been fascinated by the concept of improvement, both golf improvement and life improvement. I realized early on that there was a lot more to golf improvement than just understanding swing mechanics.

It's one thing to *know* something, but it's another thing to *do* what you know. For example, you may know that it's best to swing your club on an inclined swing plane, but do you? You may know that it's best to stay relaxed when you play, but are you?

If you've ever had the thought, "I know what I'm doing wrong, but I just can't seem to fix it!" you know exactly what I'm talking about. Having a change go from the level of understanding to the level of "owning" (i.e., doing it automatically) is what practice is all about.

Ever since I started presenting golf seminars over 20 years ago, I've had a pet project. I've talked with golfers on driving ranges, short game areas, and practice putting greens all over the country, and asked them a very simple question, "What are you practicing?"

> # My Pet Project
>
> ## I've asked golfers all over the country, "What are you practicing?"

Well, at least I thought it was a simple question. The answers have been quite enlightening, often surprising, and dare I say, entertaining at times, too!

After asking hundreds of golfers my patented question, "What are you practicing?" here are the top three things I discovered:

1. Most golfers have no idea what they're practicing.

Coach Dori – "What are you practicing?"
Golfer – "My swing."
Coach Dori – "Can you be more specific?"
Golfer – "I'm working on getting more distance."
Coach Dori – "How exactly are you doing that?"
Golfer – "Like I told you, I'm working on my swing!"

Like most golfers I've asked, this golfer had no idea what he was practicing. He knew the *result* he wanted, but he had no idea of the specific change that was required to achieve that result.

If he continued to practice this same way for 10 hours a week, how many months do you think it would take him to reach his goal? I hope you realize this is a trick question because he could practice this way for the rest of his life and never see a permanent improvement to his distance!

2. Some golfers have a vague idea of what they're practicing.

Coach Dori – "What are you practicing?"
Golfer – "I'm trying to straighten out my slice."
Coach Dori – "Are you working on anything specific?"
Golfer – "My backswing."
Coach Dori – "What are you trying to change?"
Golfer – "I want to make a bigger turn."
Coach Dori – "Could you show me what you mean?"
Golfer – "Well, I'm not exactly sure, but I think I'm supposed to do something like this [demonstrates one turn, then demonstrates another]."

Some golfers do have a vague idea of what they're practicing, but it's not nearly specific enough for the change to become permanent.

It's like "the angry man in Des Moines." He was an attendee at a golf school that had scheduled me to present a two-hour evening seminar. I came early to meet the participants and I saw this man at the end of the range visibly frustrated.

I approached him respectfully, wanting to learn more, and asked him what he was practicing. He spent the next five minutes trying to show me, as he pounded golf ball after golf ball, getting more and more frustrated.

In the end, all I could gather was that it had something to do with his backswing. He couldn't say because he didn't know; he just knew it wasn't working.

Unbelievable as it might sound, he was extremely angry with himself because he couldn't do what he wanted, but he didn't even know what he wanted to do!

3. Many golfers are practicing a list of vague things.

> Coach Dori – "What are you practicing?"
> Golfer – "I'm working on my alignment, keeping my head down, keeping my left arm straight, improving my weight shift, delaying my release, slowing down my swing, and finishing in balance."
> Coach Dori – (speechless)

> ## "A journey of any length begins with a single step."
>
> *Adaptation of Lao Tzu's*
> *famous saying*

What Are You Practicing?

If you think I'm exaggerating, I'm not. Next time you're at the driving range, start a casual conversation with a nearby golfer and ask them what they're practicing. Most golfers have no idea what they're practicing, or at best, they have a vague idea. Many golfers have an entire list of things they're working on.

What about you? Think back to the last time you were at the driving range. If I had walked up to you and asked, "What are you practicing?" how would you have answered?

What were you thinking about before hitting each ball? Did you have one goal in mind or did you have a list of things you were trying to accomplish? Was each goal vague or specific? Could you clearly describe how the "new way" you were practicing was distinctly different from your "old way?"

To successfully move your game from where it is now to where you want it to be, you must be SPECIFIC about the change you want to make. Equally important, you need to choose the step that will give you the most improvement.

Choosing the Right Step

There are many possible changes you could make to your golf game. We've covered several in this book – mental changes and physical changes, swing optimization changes and swing mechanics changes, small changes and big changes.

To improve in the fastest, easiest way possible, you need to find the ONE change that will move you the closest to where you want to be (i.e., the BIGGEST STEP you can take right now).

Think of Every Change as a Separate Step

Thinking of golf improvement as a series of simple steps has many benefits. For example, it:

- Helps you become more specific.
- Reminds you that each change takes time.
- Makes your improvement choices more distinct.
- Prevents you from jumping from one tip to the next.
- Reduces the number of things for you to think about.
- Helps you focus on the most important things first.
- Makes it easier to identify the time required.
- Improves the productivity of your practice.
- Provides you with a clear beginning and end.
- Gives you something to celebrate once complete!

So, what do you want most?

If you were looking at a menu that included every golf goal you could ever want and you had to pick just one, what would it be?

- More distance?
- Straighter shots?
- More consistency?
- Lower scores?
- More fun?
- Fewer 3-putts?
- More up and downs?
- Fewer topped chip shots?
- A golf swing that doesn't hurt?
- (Something else?)

Whatever goal you choose, use it as the starting point to hone in on the best step to take. For example:

- If "more distance" is your primary goal, the right step for you is the one that will increase your distance the most.

- If "straighter shots" is your primary goal, the right step for you is the one that will help you hit the straightest.

- If "more consistency" is your primary goal, the right step for you is the one that will improve your consistency the most.

- If "lower scores" is your primary goal, the right step for you is the one that will improve the aspect of your game that is costing you the most strokes.

- If "more fun" is your primary goal, the right step for you is the one that will add the most fun to your game.

You get the idea.

Once you've narrowed down the aspect of your game you want to change, review what we covered earlier in the book to decide your plan.

For example, if "more distance" is your goal, you are looking for the one change that will increase your distance the most. Using what you've learned in this book, you know that your distance is based on your CONTACT and clubhead SPEED.

So, first you would evaluate your contact. If your contact needs improvement, then you would use the information we covered in Chapter 9 to determine the specific step to take.

Work On the Most Important Changes First

Like a sculptor, it's important to start with the big changes first, and then move to the detail work.

Unfortunately, I often see golfers trying to perfect their setups and backswings before they can even consistently get the ball airborne. In this case, contact is the bigger priority and should be changed first.

It doesn't matter if you are a recreational golfer or a touring professional; there is always one change that is most important – the BIGGEST step you can take.

If you choose the most important changes first, each step you take will be a GIANT step toward your most important goals!

> # Take the time to choose the right step, and you won't waste hours practicing the wrong things!

If your contact is fine and you decide that clubhead speed is your main issue, then you would use the information we covered in Chapter 12 to choose your best step. Specifically, you might choose to create a better power angle, or to release your power angle through impact more effectively.

Of course, if "more distance" really is your number one goal and you occasionally have the distance you want, the first step I would recommend is to *optimize* your current swing habit (Chapters 6 and 7).

It Doesn't Take Much

After 15 years of going from one swing method to the next, my golf improvement didn't just seem difficult, at times it felt nearly impossible. Looking back, though, I can see that my problem was a result of focusing on the wrong things.

Like so many golfers I see today, I spent most of my time trying to learn swing methods that didn't fit me, and the rest of my time searching for something better.

Once you've broken free from the swing method cycle, you will realize there are very few things you need to change to see a dramatic improvement in your game. You'll notice that when you focus on the steps that matter most, it doesn't take much to see a HUGE change in your results.

One Change Can Make a HUGE Difference

A golfer came to me for a lesson because he, "continually topped the ball." From what he told me on the phone, I expected to see a horrible, jerky, tense, off-path swing.

Instead, I was amazed. He had a smooth, powerful, effortless swing motion that was beautiful to watch. There was one problem ... he did top almost every shot!

Apparently, the flawed, nearly hopeless golf swing he saw in his mind was very different from the golf swing I saw in person. I told him that he had a beautiful golf swing and there was just one change he needed to make.

He had tried many things in the past to eliminate his topping problem so I could tell that he wasn't buying the idea of a single change making a difference, but we proceeded just the same.

Without asking him to change anything about his swing – his setup, backswing, forward swing, or follow through – I showed him the simple reason why he was topping the ball. Within minutes, nearly every shot was airborne and straight. He couldn't believe it!

Despite the number of swing tips you've tried in the past, when you choose the *right step*, one change will make a HUGE difference!

What is Your First Step?

One day when you least expect it, I just might walk up to you on a driving range and ask, "What are you practicing?" If that happens, how will you answer?

To improve in the fastest, easiest way possible, you need to KNOW EXACTLY:

- What you are practicing
- How the change will benefit you
- How the "old way" and the "new way" are different

Make sure the step you choose is guaranteed to give you the results you want. And, remember to keep it SPECIFIC and MEASURABLE, so you can track your progress, and CELEBRATE your accomplishment!

Most importantly, take your time to choose the right step – the step that will give you the most improvement. Because, as I will show you in the next chapter, the real benefits come when you finish what you start.

Chapter 14

Cross the Finish Line

The Joy of Completion!

Imagine crossing the finish line at the end of a race. Heart pounding, you lean forward, stretching for the tape. Success! Your arms extend high overhead as you feel the excitement and exhilaration of the moment. It's electrifying!

Can you feel it? That's the joy of completion.

Golf improvement is about completion. It's not about how much you know, how many swing thoughts you have, how many tips you try, how many lessons you take, or how many changes you start; it's about how many changes you FINISH!

You can hit range balls 2 hours a day, 5 days a week, every month for the rest of your life and still have nothing to show for it if you don't complete the changes you start.

Every Change Has a Beginning and an End

In the last chapter, I discussed the importance of choosing the right step and making it specific. Before starting a change, however, it's also essential to know when you'll be DONE. I don't mean the day and time you'll be done. I mean how you will know when the change is complete.

What if you went to school for a degree, but the classes never ended? Or, what if you started a project that got bigger every time you worked on it? That's what it's like when you try to improve your golf game with no end in sight. Your swing "to-do" list gets longer and longer, sucking the fun out of your game as it grows.

Instead, you must know when you'll be DONE. You need to start every change with the finish line in sight and keep it in sight until you get there. Then, once you've crossed the finish line, it's important to graduate – to throw your hat in the air and shout at the top of your lungs, "YES! I'm done!"

Completion is vital! You need to know there's an end to what you're practicing and an exciting reward awaits you. You deserve the satisfaction of a job well done.

I know a change is complete when it automatically shows up on the golf course, even in competition. I often refer to this as "owning" the change.

When the change you're making feels second nature to you and it happens consistently without thinking about it, then you will know that you are done, too.

How Many Changes Can You Make at Once?

If I toss you a ball, most likely you will catch it quite easily. If I toss you another ball, then another, and another, one ball at a time, you should be able to catch them all with no problem.

However, what would happen if I tossed you all 5 balls at once? How many of them would you catch? Maybe one or two, but certainly not all 5, right!

Similar to catching one ball at a time, success is easy one change at a time. Each step needs and deserves your full attention.

How Long Does It Take to Make a Change?

In 2005, I was one of four speakers at a workshop for some of the top LPGA teaching professionals in the country. With over 500 years of teaching experience in the room, I asked, "How long does it take to change a habit?"

There were several different answers including, "21-days," "28-days," and "5000 repetitions." After some discussion, the overall agreement was that most swing changes take at least a month, and major changes can take over a year.

No one knows exactly how long a change will take for YOU. The only thing you can know for sure is that every change requires a commitment of time.

If I knew the specific change you wanted to make, how fast you learned, how much practice time you would commit, and how effectively you practiced, I could estimate how long it would take.

The fact is, though, some changes take longer than others. Some people learn faster than others. And, some golfers practice more effectively than others. Since even you won't know *exactly* how long your change will take, what's important is that you commit to finishing it … giving yourself all the time you need.

A change to your golf game, like a tiny oak tree sprout, will grow up to be strong and beautiful as long as you keep it in a safe, nurturing environment, and give it the time it needs to grow.

> # "An eagle trying to catch two rabbits will catch neither."
>
> *Old saying – origin unknown*

Will You Make a Change?

Years ago, I read an article in a major golf magazine, written by a famous PGA Tour Professional. He wrote that most golfers make no significant changes to their swings after they've played golf for a year.

I was a young teaching pro at the time, and I couldn't believe how *negative* the tour pro's statement was. How could he say that people who golfed for over a year wouldn't improve their swings? Didn't he know the impact his comments could have on my livelihood?

Over time, I learned that what he said was true. He wasn't being negative; he was simply stating a fact.

For most golfers, starting a swing change is like making a New Year's Resolution – at first you're highly motivated, excited about the change, and ready to do whatever it takes. Then, over time, something shifts, and you settle back to your old ways.

Over 95% of golfers who start swing changes don't complete them. Not only do they fail to achieve their goals, they waste the time and effort they invested. Just like the perfect golf swing, "follow through" is essential.

Train Your Brain With
Patience and Persistence

There was a man who really loved golf but he wasn't happy with how he was playing. One day he was reading a well-known golf magazine, and he came upon an article based on a study of the world's best golfers.

The researchers discovered that nearly 100% of the best golfers in the world put their pants on right leg first. It had something to do with how their brains worked.

After giving it some thought, the man realized he always put his pants on left leg first. Immediately, he decided to make a change so he could become a better golfer.

As you might imagine, the next morning, when he grabbed his pants, he started putting them on left leg first. Luckily, he caught himself in time, lowered his left leg, and put his right leg in first.

This went on for a few days. He would start to put his left leg in first, but he'd catch himself, stop, and put his right leg in first, instead.

After about a week, he wasn't lifting his left leg anymore. He still had to consciously stop and think about it, but it was getting easier to put his right leg in first. After three to four weeks, he was putting his pants on right leg first without even having to think about it.

The man was very pleased with his progress and decided to enjoy a fun reward. He parked himself on the couch in his favorite boxer shorts, surrounded himself with drinks and snacks, and settled in to watch a big game.

The game hadn't been on long, when suddenly his fire alarm went off. RING! RING! RING! Immediately, he jumped up and ran to grab his pants so he could get dressed before running outside. In his haste to leave safely, which leg do you think he put in first?

If you said, "left leg," you are correct! Even though his new habit had been showing up every morning for the past several weeks, when under stress, his old left leg habit was still the one his brain knew best.

Are you wondering what this has to do with your golf swing? A lot! In the beginning, you will need to stop and consciously think about the change you want to make. Over time though, it will become easier and easier to see the change without having to think about it.

And, even when your new swing starts showing up regularly on the driving range, it may still be a while before it begins showing up regularly on the golf course, where your mental "fire alarms" may go off.

Lesson to Be Learned: Be patient with yourself while making a swing change. And, more importantly, be persistent and trust that your new habit will eventually win out ... even under stress!

Specifically, schedule time for practice. Just like learning to play the piano, you can't expect improvement without devoting hours to practice.

You also have to expect that there will be some rough times. Some practice days are better than others. Sometimes scores go up before they go down. And, the familiar feeling of your old swing may try to lure you back.

When the going gets rough, remind yourself that it's a natural part of the process. Keep your eye on the goal, find a way to stay motivated, and stick with every change until you "own" it.

The Top 10 Reasons Golfers Don't Stick With a Change

1. They don't schedule enough time for practice.

2. They don't see an immediate improvement.

3. Their swing temporarily gets worse.

4. The change doesn't feel right.

5. They try to learn too many things at once.

6. They don't know how long it takes to change a habit.

7. They hear about something they think will work better.

8. The change doesn't instantly show up on the course.

9. They're confused about what they need to change.

10. They get side-tracked testing new swing tips.

What Do Piano Lessons and Custom-Fitting Your Golf Swing Have in Common?

If you've ever had piano lessons, you know how important it is to practice between lessons. If you don't practice, you don't progress, because each new skill depends on mastering the previous.

Like successful pianists, when you custom-fit your golf swing, you hone your skills progressively. So, be sure to schedule time for practice, and finish what you start before going to the next step!

Get Off the Tip Train!

Time isn't the only reason golfers don't stick with a change until completion. Golf tips are also to blame – not the tips themselves, but the false belief that accompanies them.

Take a good look at how you currently approach swing improvement. How often do you try the latest swing tips, and how long are you willing to stick with an idea before moving onto something else?

For most golfers, the average life span of a swing tip is from one to ten range balls. "Practice" becomes more about trying swing tips than making permanent swing changes. If one tip doesn't produce immediate results, it's onto the next one.

Golf tips often sound so easy. For example, "To hit longer, straighter shots, just stay in balance and release your club through impact using your ideal tempo."

Sounds easy, doesn't it? How long do you think it would take to complete – a day or two, maybe a week at the most? In actuality, that one "tip" is directing you to focus on balance, release, and tempo. Improving those three aspects of anyone's golf swing could easily take six months of effective practice to complete!

If you're serious about improvement, stop trying all the swing tips that come your way. Either turn a tip into a step and actually complete it, or let it go.

What Can I Try This Week?

Years ago, I was employed as an assistant golf professional at a Private Country Club, along with several other professionals. Whenever a new issue of a major golf magazine was released, we held a contest.

Since we were always sure that at least a few of the members would be trying out the latest swing advice, we'd get together in the pro shop to watch them hitting balls on the driving range. The winner was the first pro to figure out the featured topic of the latest issue.

Lesson to Be Learned: Read whatever you want about golf, but don't go out and try everything you read. Choose your one most important step and stick with it until it's COMPLETE. You owe it to yourself and your game!

One Step a Month, That's All I Ask

The most effective way to ensure you'll finish every change you start is to focus on ONE CHANGE A MONTH.

That may not sound like much, but it is! Just imagine how much better your game would be if you made 12 significant changes over the next year.

Or, if you live in a climate where the golf season is shortened, you could devote the off-season for habit changes, and spend the rest of the year enjoying the game and the swing you have. Imagine what a HUGE difference even six significant changes could make.

Regardless of how many changes you make in the next year, one change a month will result in a DRAMATIC improvement to your game!

Break Large Steps Into Small Steps

If you know a change will take more than 30-days to complete, simply break it into a series of small steps that can each be completed within a month. It will keep you on track and give you something to celebrate at the end of each month!

One Change a Month Not Enough?

If you think one step at a time isn't going to cut it, you can choose to work on two or three steps a month.

Beware though. It's very easy to be overly optimistic about your time. So, when working with multiple steps, prioritize them and always practice "Step 1" first.

No matter how many steps you work on each month, give every change the full time and attention it deserves!

So, What's It Going to Be?

If you are serious about improving your game, focus on one change a month, and finish what you start. Transform useful golf tips into "steps," and reward yourself for every step you complete.

Your golf swing can be as good as you want it to be. Invest your time in the *right things* and you'll see *real results*. The key is to stay focused on the one most important change you need to make and stick with it until you cross the finish line.

Chapter 15

The
Secret to
Your Success

It Really Is Easy!

I've seen it proven time and time again. If you want to improve your golf game in the fastest, easiest way, all you need to do is complete one step a month.

Completing one step at a time is probably very different than what you're used to, but if you haven't been improving as fast as you'd like, that's a good thing!

By taking time in the beginning to choose the one step that's most important, you'll save hundreds of hours in the long run, and you can feel confident that you're taking a BIG step in the right direction.

This is Different

Through the years, thousands of golfers have asked me to help them improve their swings. Sometimes, while swinging in a new way, a student will stop, look at me with a shocked expression, and say, "That feels different!"

It tickles me when students appear to be sincerely surprised that their golf swings feel different, even though they paid for golf lessons to change their swings. It's as if they believed they could get different results by continuing to do the exact same things!

If you want better results than you've been getting, you need to do something different than you've been doing.

I'm showing you a much more effective way to approach your golf swing and your practice – something I've been studying for over 20 years. Naturally, this approach will be different than what you're accustomed to, because if you want better results, you should expect a different, more effective approach.

> ## "Insanity is doing the same thing over and over again and expecting different results."
>
> Albert Einstein

There are approximately 25 million golfers in the United States. Despite the game's tremendous gain in popularity, that statistic has remained relatively unchanged for several years now. How is that possible?

The sad fact is, for the two million or so people who are taking up the game each year, two million others are giving up the game.

Something needs to change! I believe that "something" has to be a significant shift in the way we approach the golf swing and golf improvement.

In this chapter, I'm going to discuss an entirely different way to practice. It's a very important part of this book because knowing WHAT to practice is essentially useless if you don't know HOW to practice.

My Pet Project – Part 2

In Chapter 13, I told you about my pet project of asking golfers all over the country, "What are you practicing?" That was only half the story. While I was talking with golfers and asking them WHAT they were practicing, I was also studying HOW they were practicing.

Learning "how" golfers practice is a bit more difficult because it's not something they are used to talking about. So, I had to gather most of my information through observation. If I had asked golfers, "How are you practicing?" I probably would have heard a lot of, "Great, thanks!"

When I talk about "HOW you practice," I'm referring to the PROCESS of practice. For example: What is your focus? How many things are you trying to think about at once? How long are you sticking with each thought? What kind of feedback are you gathering? And so on.

After watching hundreds of golfers practice, here are the top three things I discovered about "HOW" it's usually done:

1. **Most golfers change their focus based on where the ball goes.** I call this the "Chasing Your Tail" technique.

If you do this, you might focus on ten or more different ideas while hitting the same bucket of balls. Using this technique, every time you hit a shot that doesn't go where you want, you change your thinking, hoping to solve the problem.

For example, your first swing thought is, "I need to slow down my swing." Then, you top the ball. So, next you think, "I better keep my head down." Then, you slice it. "Darn it!" you exclaim. "My club path must be going outside-in, I better swing more inside." So, you think about that. Then, you chunk it. "I must be swinging too fast," immediately comes rushing back to mind.

Around and around you go, where you'll stop nobody knows!

2. **Most golfers hit one shot after another in rapid succession.** I call this the "Rapid Fire Machine Gun" technique.

If you do this, practice is about quantity, not quality. The faster you get through the bucket, the better. Hit a good shot, drag a ball over and fire! Hit a bad shot, drag a ball over and fire! Bam! Bam! Bam! You can't hit the balls fast enough.

"Whew! I'm done," you think to yourself. "I'm glad I had time to practice." The only problem is, you didn't practice!

3. **Most golfers care more about where the ball goes than about their swing change.** I call this the "Swinging in the Dark" technique.

If you do this, you may start out with a swing goal in mind, but by the end of the swing, all you can think about is where your ball went. For example, you start with the thought, "I want to focus on my club path." Then, you set up to the ball and swing. Suddenly, all you can think about is, "Which way did it go? Which way did it go?"

You have no idea what happened with your club path, but you know exactly where the ball went!

**How effective is your practice?
Are you actually practicing,
or just hitting balls?**

The Ideal Practice R-R-Routine

Finding time in your busy schedule for practice may be difficult, but practice itself can be extremely easy. All you need to do is follow three simple steps:

1. **Rehearse**
2. **Rate**
3. **Repeat**

Repeat after me ... "Rehearse, Rate, Repeat." "Rehearse, Rate, Repeat." Let's sing it now, "Rehearse, Rate, Repeat." "Rehearse, Rate, Repeat."

It has a ring to it, doesn't it? Well, it has the "cha-ching" to it, too. Doing it will pay off in a BIG WAY!

1. **Rehearse**
   Pick ONE thing to focus on and SEE and FEEL exactly what you'd like to happen when you hit the ball. You can rehearse mentally and/or physically. The key is to show yourself EXACTLY what you want – a "10" on a scale from 1 to 10.

2. **Rate**
   Hit a ball and compare that swing to your perfect "practice swing." In other words, evaluate how closely your "ball swing" matched your perfect "10" rehearsal swing.

3. **Repeat**
   Do steps 1 and 2 again.

To achieve any swing goal, simply follow this 3-step process until you are consistently doing what you want without having to think about it.

The Ideal Practice R-R-Routine

Rehearse   Rate   Repeat
Rehearse   Rate   Repeat
Rehearse   Rate   Repeat

Does that sound easy, or what?! Well, it really is, but it might take some getting used to because you may be forced to deal with an ineffective practice habit.

For example, to "Rehearse" you must:

- Choose only one thing to practice at a time (not 2 or 3).
- Stop between balls and do a perfect "10" mentally and/or physically (no "Rapid Fire Machine Gun").

To "Rate" you must:

- Focus on your desired swing change and ignore anything that isn't directly related (no "Swinging in the Dark").

To "Repeat" you must:

- Stick with the one change you're making (no "Chasing Your Tail").

The biggest challenge for most golfers is to rate each shot. This requires being "present" while swinging.

If rating your shots ever seems difficult to you, just be patient. Stick with it, and make the commitment to increase your awareness, because the better you get at rating, the faster you'll see results!

The Missing Link

From the title of this chapter, and from what you've read so far, you may think that the "secret to your success" is practicing the "right way." Well, technically that's true. But, the real secret to success is AWARENESS!

You need FEEDBACK. Without it, you'll just keep doing the same thing over and over again. Awareness is the missing link in golf improvement. It provides the feedback you MUST have, and it gives you the power to literally shave months off your practice time.

"Awareness" is knowing exactly what is happening when you swing. It's what allows you to accurately *rate* each shot. It tells you how you are doing in relation to your goal.

Feedback is the GOLD waiting to be mined in every practice swing. It is the information you need to progress toward your goal. Without it, the chances of making a permanent swing change are slim to none.

Unfortunately, there's a strong chance you haven't been getting the feedback you need. The number one reason is because your focus has been on "sending" information instead of "receiving" it.

Sending Versus Receiving

When practicing, you have two choices. You can either *tell* yourself what to do, or *notice* what you're doing. These are very different processes. One is *sending* information and the other is *receiving* information.

If you've ever heard the phrase, "God gave me two ears and one mouth because it's twice as important to listen than it is to speak," the same applies to practice. It's much more important to receive information (illustration 15-1).

Sending vs. Receiving

No   **YES!**

Sending = trying, telling yourself, directing,
closed, hard, tense, work

Receiving = noticing, paying attention, present,
open, easy, relaxed, fun

Your brain is very good at both sending and receiving information. However, you cannot effectively receive information while you are consciously sending information. Consequently, it's best to do only one at a time.

For example, if you are in the process of swinging and you consciously tell yourself to shift your weight, you are *sending* information. That means you are not open to *receiving* information at the same moment.

After the swing, if I asked you, "How would you rate your weight shift?" you would probably look at me with a blank expression on your face as you searched for an answer. Unfortunately, you wouldn't find one because you were too busy telling yourself what to do.

When you consciously tell yourself how to swing, you don't receive feedback about what is actually happening *while* you swing. It's a bit like a walkie-talkie. You can either talk, or you can listen, but you can't do both at the same time.

To Get Feedback, You Need to "Receive"

For you to rate your practice swing (Step 2 of the "Ideal Practice R-R-Routine"), you need feedback. To get feedback, you need to stay in "receiver" mode.

That means, starting today, no more telling yourself how to swing *while* you're swinging. Instead, rehearse what you want, then swing, and NOTICE what actually happened. Just put on a detective hat and become an objective observer.

After each shot, the question isn't, "Did I do it?" The question is, "What exactly did I do?" Even if you didn't accomplish a "10," as long as you know what you *actually* did during the swing, your brain will make the necessary adjustments.

The "Did I Do It?" Lady

As a new golf instructor, I had the pleasure of working with a woman who I now affectionately refer to as the "Did I do it?" lady.

She didn't consider herself athletic, but she was very determined to learn golf so she could spend more time with her husband.

It was her first golf lesson, and I will always remember the hopeful look on her face when, after hitting a ball, she would turn to me and ask, "Did I do it?" I would smile and enthusiastically tell her what she did or didn't do.

Then, we would repeat the process. She would hit a ball, then turn to me and ask, "Did I do it?" Again, I would answer. After every ball, she would quickly and hopefully turn to ask her patented question.

She was happy and I was happy. That was ... until I saw her swing at the start of her next lesson. She hadn't improved at all!

It turns out the "Did I do it?" lady had absolutely no idea what she was doing when she swung.

From then on, instead of immediately answering her question, I showed her how to answer the question for herself. As her awareness grew, her swing improvement increased right along with it!

You need to be 100% committed to receiving when you swing ... almost as if your life depended on it. Obviously it doesn't, but your golf game certainly does!

You'll also be happy to know that receiving is much easier and more relaxing than sending. Constantly telling yourself what to do is hard work! In receiver mode, there is no judgment: no rights or wrongs, and absolutely no way you can fail ... unless you choose not to do it!

So, here's the routine for the next time you're at the range:

1. **Rehearse** the one thing you are practicing.
2. **Rate** your swing by comparing it to your perfect rehearsal.
3. **Repeat** the process.

What Are You Rating?

Often, during a lesson, a golfer will rehearse a perfect "10." Then, he (or she) will hit the ball exactly as rehearsed. I'll be very excited about the swing, whether or not it produced a good shot. To me, the golfer earned an "A+" because he did exactly what he practiced.

However, when looking at the golfer, it's a different story. Based on his body language, he gave himself a failing grade.

Obviously, we were rating entirely different things. I was rating the change he was practicing, and he was rating the result of his shot. Be sure you're rating the right thing!

The Slower You Go, the Faster Your Results

At first, you may find it challenging to gather good feedback. Over time though, it will get easier.

Receiving Information Makes Practice a Lot More FUN!

Before I discovered that I could improve my swing more quickly and easily by starting at impact and working back from there, the only way I knew to improve was to keep trying different swing methods.

Before I discovered that I could change my swing more quickly and easily by simply *noticing* what was actually happening when I swung, the only way I knew to practice was to tell myself what to do.

Just as starting at impact will allow you to find YOUR best swing, noticing what actually happens when you swing will give you the feedback you need to make swing changes much more quickly and easily.

Once you know what you want, you simply have to pay attention to what you're *actually* doing. Your wonderful brain will make the necessary adjustments from there.

Not only is it a lot more productive way to practice, it's also a lot more FUN!

For example, I frequently ask golfers, "How would you rate that swing?" In the beginning, because their focus is somewhere else, nearly all say, "Honestly, I don't know."

Sometimes I have to ask that same question several swings in a row before they get tired of not being able to answer. Then, they finally let go of focusing on the ball (or whatever else they were thinking) and shift their focus to the change they're making.

If this process also takes you several swings to get, don't worry about it. Just keep asking yourself, "How would I rate that swing?" until you have a solid answer.

Do the best you can and keep strengthening your commitment to receive the swing information you need, until you are POSITIVE that you're rating each swing accurately.

Want to Increase Your Awareness?

One of the best books ever written about awareness is, "The Inner Game of Golf" by Tim Gallwey. His first book "The Inner Game of Tennis" is also one of my all-time favorites. You can check out more of my "Top Picks" at:

www.NexStepGolf.com

No matter how many swings it takes, keep going until you know that the rating you give is more than just a guess.

Be patient with yourself. Sometimes, even when you are fully committed, it may take time to get the hang of it.

If, after doing your very best, you still can't tell what is happening when you swing, there is an easy solution.

Slooooow down!

HELP! I've Been Slicing for 10 Years and I Can't Stop!

If you don't know what is happening when you swing, you could end up working on the same thing for years and still not see any change, as this true story will illustrate.

A man called for a lesson because he had a "big problem." "I've been swinging outside-in for over ten years. I just can't seem to stop coming across the ball. It's especially bad with my driver. Sometimes I slice the ball two fairways over.

"I've taken lessons from more golf professionals than I care to count, including some of the most well-known coaches in the world. I've spent thousands of dollars on lessons, books, tapes, and training aids. I've hit thousands and thousands of range balls, and I still can't stop swinging across the ball. I need help!"

He went on to describe his problem in perfect detail. He told me exactly what was happening with his swing and how he wanted it to change.

After listening to his story, I paused, and then asked him an unexpected question.

"How is that possible?" I asked.

"How is what possible?" he responded.

(continued from previous page)

"How is it possible that you could be so clear about what you want to happen, devote hundreds of hours to practice, and still not see any change?" He looked at me, puzzled.

"Apparently, you already know what you're doing wrong, and you already know what you should be doing right. What can I possibly do for you that the other 10 or 20 golf pros haven't been able to do?"

I knew I could help him, but I wanted him to realize this lesson wouldn't be like the others. "I'm not sure," he said.

After waiting a few moments for effect, I said, "Well, I have some good news. I know I can help you in a way no one else has because there's only one way a person could know so much, yet change so little."

His interest was peaked. "What's that?" he asked.

"With all the lessons you've taken, and all the practice you've done, there's obviously one very important thing you've been missing – your awareness of what is *actually* happening when you swing."

"You can't change something you're not aware of. Just because you can talk about it doesn't mean you're aware of it WHILE it's happening."

By the end of our lesson, for the first time ever, he was aware of what his club was actually doing. In less than one month, his swing was right on path!

That may mean slowing down your swing, shortening it, or taking a shorter club. Do whatever it takes. Bottom line, you need feedback. If you don't know what is happening when you swing, SLOW DOWN and find out.

In Golf, It's Better to Receive!

To change your swing in the fastest, easiest way, you need a clear goal and feedback directly related to that goal.

In life, it may be better to give than to receive. But, in golf, receiving is where it's at!

Pay attention to what is actually happening when you swing and your brain will "magically" move you toward your most exciting golf goals.

Time for a Change

You've done it. Somehow you've found a way to clear some time in your busy schedule, and you're standing on the driving range preparing to practice. Now, it's time to "GO FOR IT!"

Make sure your practice time actually pays off with results. Be different –

- **Rehearse**
- **Rate**
- **Repeat**

Do it over and over and over again. Your awareness will continue to increase and you'll get the feedback you need to cross the finish line in style!

Chapter 16

It Doesn't Get Any Easier Than This

Golf Improvement at Its Core

The first 15 chapters of this book have shown you why approaching golf improvement in the traditional way makes it extremely difficult to get the results you want. They've also presented several effective ways to make golf improvement easier.

I used to jump from one swing method to the next, searching for the "right way" to swing. Now, I know that no swing method can show me MY best way to swing. Instead of trying to fit into "someone else's" swing method, I know the right way for me to swing is the way that is easiest and most comfortable for my body.

That realization, itself, has already saved me years of practice time that I would have spent on learning and testing new swing methods. And, that's only one of the ways I've streamlined my improvement.

Now, I know that *optimizing* my current swing habit is often a much better use of my time than *changing* my swing mechanics. And, instead of jumping from one swing thought to the next looking for a quick fix, I now practice with a single goal in mind and stick with it until I cross the finish line.

I shutter to think about all the time I wasted using ineffective practice habits. Most of the things I did in an effort to *speed up* my improvement (i.e., working on several things at once, trying new things, etc.) actually *slowed down* my improvement considerably, if they benefited me at all.

Instead of wasting time on changes that don't directly affect impact, now I know that every change I make is guaranteed to give me the results I want.

> ## When you practice the RIGHT THINGS in the RIGHT WAY, improvement really can be EASY!

I am not tempted to search for something "better" to practice because I know there's nothing more important than the completion of the one step I've chosen.

Obviously, the way I approach golf improvement now is very different than the way I used to approach it. I think about fewer things and improve more. I see maximum results from the limited time I devote to practice, and I enjoy steady and continual improvement.

By ending your search for the "right way" to swing, optimizing your current swing habit before trying to change it, focusing on your one most important step each month, and sticking with every change until completion, you, too, can experience the joy and satisfaction that real golf improvement brings.

But, we're not done yet! In the next three chapters, I'm going to show you how to make the I-Swing System even EASIER! For starters, allow me to introduce you to the *I-Swing Coach*™, the ideal tool for the I-Swing System.

My Secret Weapon

The **I-Swing Coach**™ is the highest quality swing training bag ever developed (photos 16-1 and 16-2).

If you're already familiar with swing bags, you probably know that it's the only swing training aid that allows you to SEE and FEEL the exact position of your club and body at impact. If this is the first time you've ever heard about swing bags, you're in for a real treat.

16-1

Demonstrating the ideal club position
at impact using an I-Swing Coach™

16-2

The I-Swing Coach™ Swing Training Bag

A swing bag gives you IMMEDIATE feedback about impact. There's no other training aid like it. It's such an invaluable tool for the I-Swing System that I strongly recommend one for all my golf students, and I include one with most of my training programs.

Impact can happen so quickly, it's not always easy to gather the feedback you need. However, with an I-Swing Coach, gathering accurate feedback about impact couldn't be easier. You simply swing into the side of the bag, stop, and check the exact position of your club and body. There's no guesswork.

I use an I-Swing Coach in my own practice sessions, as well as for teaching. Let me give you a quick overview of how it works. Then, I'll walk you through some of the great ways you can use an I-Swing Coach to improve your swing more quickly and easily, too.

How the I-Swing Coach Works

The I-Swing Coach is a lightweight, portable swing training bag made with a fully opening upper lid, soft foam handle, skid-resistant bottom, water-resistant inner lining, and patented dual-density foam hitting area that combines a softer feel at impact with maximum durability.

You can use it at the driving range, in your backyard, or even in your living room – like many of my students do – as long as you have enough room to swing.

Some students also keep an extra I-Swing Coach in their trunk so they can pull it out at the golf course for a quick warm-up in the parking lot before teeing off.

The fully opening upper lid zips open and closed so you can easily fill the bag with soft materials like towels or old clothes (photos 16-3 and 16-4).

16-3

16-4

Upper lid fully open for easy access, the I-Swing Coach is ready to be filled.

Fill the I-Swing Coach with towels, clothes, or other soft materials.

The I-Swing Coach™ Story

Swing bags have been around for years. They are one of the most popular swing training aids of all time.

The first swing bag I purchased didn't even last one day before the seams split. The second one was less than two weeks old when the same thing happened.

At $40 a pop, that was an expensive habit so I decided to get creative and test some other options. The best thing I could find was a heavy-duty canvas bag, but with the force of a golf swing, it split almost immediately.

Then, God smiled on me. One day, a golf student picked up my old bag (covered with so much silver duct tape you could barely see the original color) and after close inspection, he began explaining why the seams had split so easily.

I was quite intrigued by what he said, and approximately three years later – after hours of rigorous testing and numerous prototypes – the I-Swing Coach™ was born!

Thanks to my golf student's manufacturing expertise and patented "dual-density foam" technology – a softer, more flexible foam for better feel in the hitting area, melded with a denser, more rigid foam for increased support and durability – combined with some of my ideas about how to make the bag more user-friendly, together we created the highest quality swing bag ever made!

The I-Swing Coach Represents Impact

The primary goal of the I-Swing Coach is to simulate impact. Therefore, it's best to set up to the bag exactly as you would to a golf ball.

For example, if you normally play a pitching wedge in the middle of your stance, position your body so your club will contact the bag in the middle of your stance (photo 16-5).

16-5

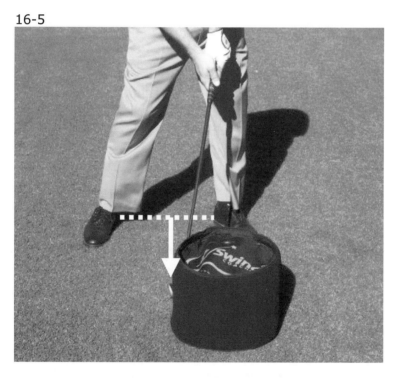

Set up to your I-Swing Coach™
so your club contacts the bag where
you would normally play the ball.

> # In the old days, before swing bags were invented, some golf professionals were known to hit against old tires.

You can swing into the I-Swing Coach with any golf club – wood, iron, or wedge. Simply change your relationship to the bag when using different clubs the same way you would adjust your stance to the ball.

For example, if you set-up with the ball forward in your stance when swinging longer clubs, set up to the I-Swing Coach with the contact point forward in your stance when practicing with longer clubs.

Set Up Your Club Just Below Middle

Many golfers automatically set up to the I-Swing Coach with their club resting on the ground, similar to where they would normally position it for a golf shot.

However, there are two problems with this:

1. If you start with your club resting on the ground and you swing back to the same spot at the bottom of the bag, your club will tend to swing under the bag, preventing you from seeing the clubface and getting the feedback you need.

2. If you start with your club resting on the ground and you swing it UP into the middle of the I-Swing Coach, this low to high motion will give you incorrect feedback because you'll be starting at one spot and ending at another.

The correct place to position your clubhead is just below the middle of your I-Swing Coach (photo 16-6).

Since you are starting with your clubhead higher than usual, you may also find that you will stand a bit farther from the bag to assume your standard arm extension. Other than that, once you've placed your clubhead against the side of the bag, simply take your normal setup position.

I've NEVER seen the higher clubhead position cause any problems with contact. However, I have talked with golfers who were concerned about it. If the higher starting point concerns you in any way, simply grip down on the club or stand on a higher level than the bag to adjust for the increase in height (photo 16-7).

16-6

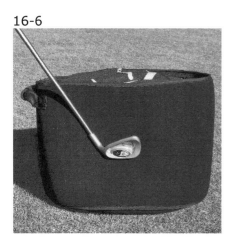

16-7

Set up with your clubhead just below the middle of the I-Swing Coach.

To make the middle of the bag comparable to ground height, stand higher than the bag.

Anchor Your I-Swing Coach

Before using an I-Swing Coach, be sure to "anchor it" by placing it against something solid.

Golfers have been very creative about what they use to anchor their bag:

- Trees

- Fences

- Benches

- Patio posts

- Range space dividers

- Golf cart tires

- Bag stands

- Golf bags

- Couches and chairs (do so at your own risk! ☺)

If you don't anchor your I-Swing Coach, it will slide each time you hit it. You will then have to reposition yourself or the bag. When this happens over and over again, it can get old real fast!

So, anchor your I-Swing Coach against a stable object, and you're ready to practice.

Allow the I-Swing Coach to Capture Your Club

I recommend starting with a very SLOW swing speed and working up from there. The goal is to find a comfortable speed that allows your club to be "captured" by the bag.

The tendency for many golfers is to hit the bag with maximum power. The goal is NOT to see how far you can hit your bag, or to try to swing through it. The goal is to let the bag *capture* your club so you can gather valuable feedback about impact (photo 16-8).

16-8

Allow the club to be captured by the bag

Step 1 - Master the Ideal Club Position

Regardless of your swing goal, the first thing to do when using an I-Swing Coach is to make sure you are swinging into the ideal impact position.

For our purposes here, I'll assume you want to hit a straight shot. So, what you're looking for at impact is a:

- Square clubface
- Club shaft tilted toward your target

There are two quick ways to check if your club shaft is tilted toward your target. After swinging into the bag, freeze your position, then:

16-9

1. Notice if the grip end of your club is pointing toward your front underarm

2. Notice if a line could be drawn along your front arm and club (photo 16-9)

As you can see, the "line" between your front arm and club is actually bowed slightly toward the target, but most golfers refer to it as "straight," as I will.

Check for a "straight" line between your front arm and club.

If you look at pictures of golf professionals at impact, no matter how differently they swing, every one of them arrives at impact with this same "straight line" relationship between their front arm and club.

There's No Way to Fail

It doesn't matter how you do it. You can swing any way you want. There's no time limit. The only requirement is that you swing your club into the bag and stop after every swing to check the position of your club at impact.

You have only one goal – to get your club into the proper position at impact. At first, it's very likely that your club won't be in the ideal position at impact. That's perfectly okay ... and also quite normal!

If your club is not in the correct position (clubface square and tilted toward your target), simply move your club where you want it to be and hold that position for a few seconds to give yourself the feel of it.

In other words, if your club doesn't end up in the proper position at impact, simply adjust it and get the FEEL for the correct position. Then swing again, and repeat the process.

On the next repetition, if your club ends up where you want it to be, great! If not, simply adjust it again, reminding your brain of the position you want.

Continue to repeat this process over and over until you can swing your club into the ideal impact position with ease. If you ever feel stuck, simply slow down until you experience success.

With the most important aspect of your golf swing taken care of, the next step is to find your body's best way to swing.

It Works for Annika!

In "Golf Annika's Way," Annika Sorenstam wrote:

"On the practice range, I like to simulate impact conditions by making swings into a special beanbag called an impact bag. By using this training aid, I get a better idea of where the club and my body – particularly my hips, left arm, and left leg – are at impact. That's important information, because impact is the moment in the swing that matters most." (p. 83)

From GOLF ANNIKA'S WAY by Annika Sorenstam, with the editors of Golf magazine, copyright © 2004 by Esch & Stam, Inc. Used by permission of Gotham Books, an imprint of Penguin Group (USA) Inc.

Step 2 – Find Your Body's Easiest Way

I think this is absolutely the most exciting part of the I-Swing System! With impact handled and your I-Swing Coach providing immediate feedback, you're ready to find your INSTINCTIVE SWING – the easiest, most comfortable, and most powerful swing for your body.

A short story – one I like to tell my students – will start you on the right track.

"Imagine driving through a small town, the kind you might see in the movies, with a speed trap and a crooked sheriff.

"Anyway, you get pulled over and then taken to the courthouse where you learn that the sheriff is also the judge and the mayor. Of course, you are found guilty. However, the good news is, you are given three options.

"You can choose between a $10,000 fine, a week in jail, or hitting a swing bag for eight hours. You don't want to pay the money, and you want to get out of town as quickly as possible, so you choose the bag.

"You're handed a golf club and told there are only two requirements. Every time you hit the bag, you must make a full swing and your club has to end up in the required position at impact. Otherwise, you can swing any way you want.

"Since you play golf, you start using your regular golf swing. But, after about five minutes, your body reminds you that you have to hit this bag for eight hours. You quickly realize you had better figure out an easier way to swing or your body won't make it!

"So, you start experimenting with different ways to swing. Since you can swing any way you want as long as you take a full swing and reach the proper position at impact, there's no need to expend any more energy than necessary.

"You give yourself a single goal – to find the motion that's most comfortable for your body – because you do have to hit this bag for eight full hours!"

The Secret to Finding Your Best Swing

As you have probably guessed by now, my point with this story is to free you up to hit the bag any way you want. I certainly don't want you limiting yourself to your current swing habit.

The secret is ... THINK IMPACT! Pretend you will hit your I-Swing Coach for eight full hours and find your body's easiest way to get the club where it needs to be at impact.

For New Golfers Only

I've shown brand new golfers, who had never held a golf club before, how to use the I-Swing Coach. They've gotten the feel of a great swing and hit some wonderful airborne and straight shots in less than 10-minutes.

Because the bag stops your swing at impact, as a new golfer, it's also important to practice swinging into a balanced finish position so you can get the feel of a complete swing (without using the bag or hitting balls). Ideally, almost all of your weight will be on your front leg and your upper body will be rotated toward the target (photo 16-10 below).

16-10

> # The secret to finding YOUR best swing is ...
> # THINK IMPACT!

Whatever you do, don't try to swing the "right way." Find your body's *easiest* way. With 7 hours and 55 minutes to go, is there any other way to swing that might be easier? If you could swing any way you wanted (because you can), how would you do it?

Remember, your club and body are already where they need to be at impact, so there's no chance you're swinging the wrong way. Now, it's time to find the easiest way!

You have 7 hours, 45 minutes to go. That's a really long time to make a motion that doesn't feel good. So, let go of any excess tension. Streamline any unnecessary motions. And, find the swing that feels the best and requires the least amount of effort.

You have 7 hours, 30 minutes to go. If I were you, I'd keep experimenting until I found something even easier. Remember, there's no "right way" to swing – just the easiest and most comfortable way for YOUR BODY.

It's All About YOU!

As you let go of all the uncomfortable positions, unnecessary motions, and muscle-grabbing tension, an unbelievably powerful, efficient, consistent, rhythmic, smooth, and beautiful golf swing will begin to emerge.

If your swing has felt awkward and robotic, if you've seriously contemplated giving up golf because you've lost almost all hope of having a repeatable or workable swing, or if you've been struggling with your golf swing in any way, the revelation that an incredibly wonderful golf swing has been inside you all along can be a life-changing experience!

For a coach, the looks on the golfers' faces, the statements they make, and their tears of joy are absolutely priceless.

"You mean I don't have to hold the club that way? It's always hurt my hands!"

"Are you saying I don't have to stand that way? It's been killing my back!"

"You mean I don't have to think about that list of swing thoughts anymore? This is so much more relaxing!"

Perhaps for the first time ever, you'll be in charge of your golf swing. You'll be deciding what feels best. Instead of trying to follow someone else's version of right and wrong, you'll be taking the reins on your swing and deciding which positions and motions are right and wrong for YOU, based on how they feel to YOU.

The results will be absolutely amazing!

Step 3 – Follow the Ideal Practice R-R-Routine

Once you've discovered your body's best way to swing – your Instinctive Swing – then it's time to actually learn it.

The idea of "learning" your Instinctive Swing may seem a bit strange because you already know what it feels like. However, when you set up to a golf ball right now and ask your brain to play the mental tape called "Golf Swing," your usual way of swinging will automatically play.

Your Instinctive Swing has not yet become your current swing habit. For this to happen, practice is essential. Specifically, you need to pay attention to what happens when you strike a golf ball, and increase your awareness until your ball-striking swing is identical to your bag swing.

The easy, powerful, and consistent swing you felt when hitting the I-Swing Coach is your "Ideal Swing Model." It's your "10" on a scale from 1 to 10.

Once you know your "10" swing, then choose the ONE most important change you want to make and follow the "Ideal Practice R-R-Routine" previously discussed:

- Rehearse
- Rate
- Repeat

To better understand how to transfer your "10" swing from the I-Swing Coach to the ball, here are three specific examples of how the process works.

* Example 1 *
Improving Your Tempo

1. Rehearse

Take several swings into
your I-Swing Coach to
establish a good flow
(photo 16-11).

When your swing feels
great, notice the tempo
of your swing. That is
your "10."

2. Rate

Within a few seconds of
feeling your "10" with the
I-Swing Coach, set up to
a golf ball and swing.

16-11

Take several swings
into the I-Swing Coach
to establish a good flow.

Pay full attention to your tempo. How was your tempo in
relation to your practice swing with the bag? Was the
backswing slower? Was your forward swing faster? Was
your entire swing faster than your practice swing?

Don't *try* to make your tempo the same as with the bag –
that's "sending." Simply *notice* the tempo you ACTUALLY
had during the swing – stay open to "receiving."

If your swing was a blank and all you can report on is where
the ball went, you lost a great opportunity. But, don't worry;
you will get another chance with the next ball. Simply stay
focused on learning what is actually going on when you
swing, and your awareness will continue to increase.

When you can confidently report on your tempo, whether you rated it a "3" or a "10," you get an A+!

3. Repeat

If you got a "3," excellent! Way to notice! If you got a "10," excellent! Jump for joy!

Either way, go back to the I-Swing Coach and capture your great-feeling tempo again. Or, if the feeling of your "10" tempo is still fresh in your mind, set up to another ball and swing again.

Repeat, repeat, repeat! Follow this ideal practice routine until your tempo shows up regularly on the golf course without having to think about it.

---

* Example 2 *
Straightening Out a Slice

---

1. Rehearse

The most common reason for a slice is an "outside-in" clubhead path. Since your club follows your arms, and your arms follow your shoulders, in addition to your clubface and shaft tilt, you will need to check your shoulder position at impact.

If you're slicing the ball due to an outside-in clubhead path, your shoulders will be "open" at impact (i.e., rotated), with your front shoulder pulled away from the target line.

To counteract this, feel what it's like to swing into the I-Swing Coach with your shoulders square at impact – that is, parallel to the target line (photo 16-13).

16-13

"Square" shoulder position at impact

To rehearse this adjustment, simply swing into your I-Swing Coach, freeze your position, and notice your shoulder alignment.

There are several ways to check whether your shoulders are open or square:

- Remember where your shoulders were in your setup and see if they are back in that same position (parallel to the target line), or if they have rotated.

- After swinging into the I-Swing Coach, freeze your position and have a friend hold a club across the front of your shoulders.

- Practice in front of a mirror.

Once you can swing into your I-Swing Coach with your shoulders square at impact, you will know that your clubhead path is no longer "outside-in." When you can do that with a swing that feels GREAT, you will have your "10" swing to rehearse.

2. Rate

Once you've rehearsed your "10," choose one aspect of that swing directly related to your clubhead path and focus your full attention there – first in your practice swing, and then while hitting the ball.

For example, you could choose to follow the motion of your front shoulder, front forearm, front hand, or the clubhead itself. Start with the one that seems the easiest to focus on and notice exactly what happens with that one aspect in your "10" practice swing.

Then, hit a ball and rate how closely your "ball swing" matches your "bag swing," reporting only on that one aspect.

3. Repeat

Continue this process for as long as it takes, until the "10" club path you have when using the bag naturally shows up on the golf course without thought.

I suggest adding variety to your practice sessions by periodically changing the aspect of the swing you're focusing on. For example, you might focus on the motion of your front arm for 20 balls, and then your clubhead for the next 20. Remember though, focus on only one aspect per repetition.

---

* Example 3 *
Increasing Your Distance

---

1. Rehearse

I have a book that shows the swing sequences of 25 famous touring professionals, both men and women. As you might expect, each swing is as unique as the individual golfer.

At the same time, there are some important similarities at impact. For example, all the golfers have the "straight line" relationship between their front arms and clubs that we previously discussed.

The professional golfers also have:

16-14

1. More than half of their weight on their front foot

2. Their upper bodies tilted away from the target (photo 16-14)

These two body positions are commonly referred to as "shifting your weight" and "staying behind the ball." They are both signs of a powerful release.

Therefore, when increasing distance is your goal, it's also important to check for these two body positions at impact.

For maximum power, tilt your upper body away from the target.

The amount of weight you shift to your front leg and the amount of spine tilt you have at impact will be unique to you, but both will be present once you've discovered your body's most powerful way to swing.

When you can swing into the I-Swing Coach easily and effortlessly with at least half of your weight on your front leg and your spine tilted away from the target, you have found your "10" swing to rehearse.

2. Rate

Once you've used the I-Swing Coach to gain a rock solid awareness of how a powerful swing feels, then choose one aspect of that swing directly related to your release.

For example, you could choose your power angle, weight shift, clubhead path, release point, or spine tilt. Again, start with the one that seems the easiest to focus on, and notice exactly what happens with that one aspect when you take a practice swing.

Then, hit a ball and rate how closely your "ball swing" matches your "bag swing" for that one aspect.

3. Repeat

Continue this process for as long as it takes until your powerful bag swing naturally shows up on the golf course without thought.

To keep your practice sessions fresh, remember, you can focus on one aspect of your swing for several balls, then step back and focus on another aspect, as long as you keep only ONE specific goal in mind for each swing. For example, you might focus on power angle for your first 10-20 balls, then step back and focus on your release point for the next 10-20.

Freedom at Last!

The I-Swing Coach makes it easy to increase your distance because you can actually HEAR and FEEL the power you generate from one swing to the next. As the sound of impact gets louder, you will actually feel the sensation of greater power at impact.

The I-Swing Coach also makes it easy to *optimize* your current swing habit or *change* your swing mechanics by providing immediate feedback.

Most important, it's the best tool for the I-Swing System because it's the most effective way to discover your Instinctive Swing – your body's easiest, most comfortable, and most powerful way to swing!

Gathering Feedback is EASY with the I-Swing Coach!

If you want to improve your golf swing, you need feedback. The I-Swing Coach is the best tool for the I-Swing System because it's the only swing training aid that allows you to SEE and FEEL the exact position of your club and body at impact. This immediate feedback makes it easy for you to find YOUR best swing!

Chapter 17

You'll Just Keep Getting Better and Better

There's No Limit to How Good You Can Be

One of the best things about CUSTOM-FITTING your golf swing is the consistent improvement you'll experience. The longer you use the I-Swing System and I-Swing Coach, the better your swing will become.

Taking one simple step at a time, you can make your golf swing as good as you want it to be. You can keep improving for as long as you play, or you can stop at any time and enjoy the swing you have. The choice is yours.

With continued use of the I-Swing System, you will reach a point when your major swing problems are gone. Then, what will you do?

There are three primary options:

1. Enjoy the swing you have.
2. Shift your focus to swing optimization.
3. Take another step closer to your Instinctive Swing.

The third choice is the one you'll be learning about in this chapter.

The I-Swing System offers much more than just solutions to remedial swing problems. It offers you a way to find your best swing from start to finish – setup to follow through.

Imagine knowing your body's BEST way to swing – from your grip, stance, and takeaway; to your shoulder turn, weight shift, and release; all the way to your ideal finish position.

With your major swing problems solved, that's exactly what you'll discover. Every step you take will move you closer to your Instinctive Swing – your body's easiest, most comfortable, and most powerful way to swing.

It's Time to Talk About Your Body

Throughout this book, I've purposely focused on the motions and positions of your *club,* and not those of your *body*.

As I explained in Chapter 3, when golf instruction begins with the motions and positions of the body, improvement of the club position at impact is not guaranteed.

When you first use the I-Swing System, you focus on your CLUB and allow your body to do whatever feels best.

Once your club position is consistently ideal at impact, THEN

The closer you get to your Instinctive Swing, the better your swing will FEEL and the more consistent you will BE!

you are ready to take advantage of the I-Swing System to become more and more precise about your body positions.

This natural progression from club to body, and from general body positions to more specific positions, is the most effective order for swing improvement.

As long as you continue using the I-Swing System, you will reach a point when you no longer have major swing issues. That's when the time will be right to take the I-Swing System to the next level and shift your attention from your club to your body.

What is the Easiest Swing For You?

When the time is right to take one step closer to your Instinctive Swing, the first thing to do is decide which aspect of your swing to focus on.

For example, you might select ONE of the following:

SETUP
- Left hand position
- Right hand position
- Club position
- Spine tilt
- Stance width
- Alignment
- Balance

BACKSWING
- Takeaway
- Wrist cock
- Shoulder turn
- Swing plane
- Weight distribution

FORWARD SWING
- Weight shift
- Club path
- Release

Make sure your choice is specific enough to get good feedback. In other words, choose "takeaway" or "wrist cock" instead of "backswing," which is too broad.

Once you've determined the particular aspect of your swing to focus on, the next step is to set up to your I-Swing Coach and begin experimenting.

For example, if you want to find the best stance width for your body, swing into the I-Swing Coach using the narrowest stance you can manage. Then, take a slightly wider stance and swing again. Gradually widen your stance on each swing until you've gone from one end of the spectrum to the other.

You're FEELING for the ONE stance width that allows you to swing into the I-Swing Coach with the most comfort, balance, and power.

If you typically vary your stance width based on the length of club you are swinging, the I-Swing Coach is the perfect tool for experimentation. Somewhere between narrow and wide, one stance width for each club will feel better than the others.

The I-Swing System Works for New Golfers and Tour Professionals

By starting with your golf club at impact and moving from general body positions to more precise body positions, you will always focus on the one aspect of your swing that is the highest priority.

Whether you're new to golf, playing professionally, or somewhere in between, the I-Swing System starts exactly where you are, allowing you to progress at whatever pace you want, and keeping you focused on the step that matters most to your current swing.

Once you've found the stance width that feels best, compare it to the stance width you've been using. If they're the same, CONGRATULATIONS! You're already using your best stance.

If they're different, file the information away for later use, or make "stance width" the next step you take to the finish line.

You can follow this process with every aspect of your swing – grip, takeaway, release, and so on. In each case, simply use the I-Swing Coach to discover the body motion or position that allows you to reach ideal impact in the easiest, most effective way.

How I Found My Body's Best Swing

Earlier in this book, I told you the story of what led me to the development of the I-Swing System.

On page 38, I talked about "A Life-Changing Realization," and how it developed into a completely different way to approach the golf swing. On page 39, I shared how wonderful it was to have "Total Freedom" in my golf swing for the first time since I started playing golf.

The main reason I was able to experience this freedom so quickly was because I used a swing bag.

Right away, my "bag swing" felt GREAT! It felt much more natural than the golf swing I had at the time. It was so comfortable, effortless, and powerful, you would've thought I'd been swinging that way my entire life.

Get a Grip!

One day I was talking with a fairly new golfer about the I-Swing System. As part of our discussion, I happened to bring up some of the different ways to hold a club - interlocking, overlapping, and 10-finger "baseball-style."

Suddenly, his face lit up. "This feels great!" he exclaimed, grabbing a club and trying the 10-finger grip. "I didn't know I could hold the club this way! I was told that I had to hold it with my fingers interlocked. It actually hurt my hands but I didn't think there was another choice."

He was thrilled! And, I was reminded of something similar that had happened to me. I told him the story.

"As a new golfer, I was told an overlapping grip was best. I was also told that a 10-finger grip was good for weaker women so they could get extra distance, but it wasn't a good choice for men or stronger women golfers (like me)."

I laughed as I remembered. "I never wanted to use the 10-finger grip because I didn't want to be considered weak! Now I use a 10-finger grip because it feels better to my hands and gives me more power.

"I guess the same grip that makes 'weak' women hit farther can make strong women golfers hit farther, too!"

Lesson to Be Learned: The "right way" to swing is the way that feels best to YOU! Trust yourself to know.

The bag and I became inseparable practice partners. I gave myself total permission to swing any way I wanted as long as I ended up in the proper position at impact (photo 17-1).

I enjoyed experimenting with different setup positions and swing motions to find which FELT best.

I soon realized there was always ONE way that felt better than all the others. So, I challenged myself to find the ONE way that fit my body best for every aspect of my swing.

17-1

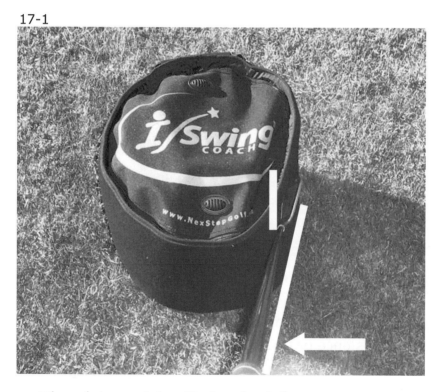

The club position I checked for at impact –
I wanted to see my clubface square and
my club shaft tilted toward the target.

> ## "I saw the angel in the marble and I carved until I set him free."
> *Michaelangelo*

Seeing and feeling that my club and body were in the right position at impact gave me the confidence I needed to experiment with everything from my grip and stance to my weight shift and release.

I focused on one aspect of my swing at a time so I could isolate how each change felt. After honing in on the best way for my body, I would challenge myself to see if I could find an even easier way.

If I felt any unnecessary motion, I streamlined it. If I felt any unnecessary tension, I released it. If I did anything that felt awkward or required excessive effort, I looked for a better way.

Discovering my Instinctive Swing was a euphoric experience. I didn't have to "teach" myself how to swing better. I knew how all along. I simply had to uncover it – to release all that it wasn't. The golf swing I had searched for, for so many years, was inside me the entire time.

Hitting balls once or twice a week, it took me about two months to find my body's best way to swing. Then I knew there was no swing anywhere that would fit me better; there was no swing easier for MY BODY!

I certainly didn't "own" my completely Instinctive Swing after those first two months. However, I did have a map to follow. I knew exactly what I wanted. And, I was ecstatic! My search for the best way to swing was finally over!

The Goldilocks Process

What helped me hone in on my best swing most was a process I developed that I affectionately named the "Goldilocks Process™."

If you recall from the old story of "Goldilocks and the Three Bears" (author unknown), when Goldilocks stumbled into the cottage of the three bears, first she tested the chairs, then the porridge, and finally, the beds.

Each time she had three choices – two that didn't work and one that was "just right." For example, Papa Bear's porridge was "too hot," Mama Bear's was "too cold," and Baby Bear's was "just right!"

When it comes to swing improvement, you also have three choices for each aspect of your swing – "too much," "too little," and "just right!"

Returning to my earlier example of stance width, you can define it even further by finding the stance width that is barely "too much" and barely "too little."

By finding the "too much" and "too little" positions, you will also have found your "just right" position.

On the next page, the photos demonstrate how the Goldilocks Process can be used to find the "ideal" spine tilt at impact – the easiest, most powerful, and most comfortable (see photos 17-2, 17-3, and 17-4).

17-2

"Too much"

17-2

"Too little"

17-4

"JUST RIGHT"

You're the Judge

Trusting yourself to know what feels best in your golf swing may be a new experience for you. Consequently, it may take a while getting used to it. However long it takes, it's certainly time well spent!

The Goldilocks Process is extremely simple and a lot of fun. Best of all, you'll find YOUR best swing – your Instinctive Swing – which means you'll get great results and a swing that feels JUST RIGHT!

Remember ...

Only YOU can judge what feels best to your body. Only YOU know what feels "JUST RIGHT." Continue to uncover the swing that is easiest, most comfortable, and most powerful for your body, and your results will keep getting better and better.

Chapter 18

Coaching for a Lifetime

Go For It!

You now have all the information you need to start custom-fitting your golf swing – today! The I-Swing System works, and this book lays out your course. All you have to do is follow it.

Which step are you going to complete first? Are you going to optimize your swing or change one of your mechanics? Do you have a physical issue that requires an immediate swing change, or are you ready to take one step closer to your Instinctive Swing?

If you have a specific swing problem you want to change, which one of the four aspects of impact will be your initial focus – contact, direction, distance, or trajectory? What is the specific change you will make?

Or, if you've been working on your swing for a long time, perhaps your first step will be to rid yourself of conscious interference. That way, you can see how good your current swing habit really is.

Whatever you want, first decide which step to complete. Pick just one. Do your best to choose the most important. Make sure you have the time required to complete it. Give yourself at least a month to get it done. Decide how you will reward yourself when you cross the finish line. Then, GO FOR IT!

As long as you choose a step that will optimize your current swing habit, change your club position at impact, or make your swing easier for your body, you can be sure you're taking a step in the right direction.

The Road to Success

Once you've chosen a step to complete over the next month, it's time to begin your journey.

Using the I-Swing System and I-Swing Coach, you will get the LOOK and FEEL of the "10" swing you want almost immediately. With that as your model, you will have the most direct path to your final destination.

What you must remember is that *feeling* the swing you want and *having* the swing you want are not the same. When you hit into the I-Swing Coach and you *feel* your "10" swing, it doesn't mean you've arrived at your final swing destination. It simply means you have a clear map to follow – an "ideal swing model" you can use as a comparison to your current swing habit.

Golf improvement is a process. There is a road you must travel. Awareness is what moves you forward. This is where practice and solid feedback come in.

As you "Rehearse-Rate-Repeat," you will become more and more aware of the difference between your "10" practice swing and your current swing habit. As your awareness increases, the gap between your present swing and your ideal swing will steadily close.

When your "ball swing" feels as natural and comfortable as your "practice swing," THEN you will have reached your final destination.

> # Take the time you need
> # to finish what you start.

You Cannot Fail!

So, you've chosen a step, you've committed to it for a month, and now the month is over. It's time to evaluate your progress. How did you do? Did you complete it? If not, how close did you come?

If the step is complete, you're DONE! It's time to celebrate. Jump for joy. Whoop it up. Give yourself a special reward. Play your favorite course. Take a day off. Buy yourself something cool. Tell yourself how wonderful you are. Get EXCITED!!!

If you're not done yet, this isn't a time for negativity, feeling bad, or for wishing you were somewhere that you're not. It's the time to acknowledge how far you've progressed and to step back and take an objective look at what happened.

For example:

- Was your goal specific enough?
- Did you rehearse a perfect "10" before each shot?
- Were you able to feel exactly what was happening when hitting balls?
- Did you practice as much as you had planned?
- Were you able to stay focused on one thing at a time?
- Did you run into any unexpected challenges?

The key is to learn everything you can about the process so you can do even better next month.

As long as you don't give up, you'll never fail. Each month, you'll either reach your destination or you'll gather valuable information. Both ways, you're making progress.

Make Sure Every Step is a S.M.A.R.T. Step

S = Specific
M = Measurable
A = Attainable
R = Realistic
T = Timely

1. Is this month's step specific and well-defined?
2. Do you have a concrete way to measure your progress?
3. Is your step small enough to complete within a month?
4. Do you have the resources and time the step requires?
5. Is this the right time to make this change?

Make Adjustments as Needed

Once you've evaluated your progress at the end of each month, make adjustments as needed.

For example:

- If your step was too broad, make it more specific by breaking it into smaller, more manageable steps.

- If you didn't stop to "rehearse" before each shot, adjust your practice routine accordingly.

- If you had trouble accurately rating your shots, strengthen your commitment to sharpen your awareness.

- If you found it difficult to stick with the one step you chose, figure out the cause and modify as needed.

- If you didn't put in the time, get creative and find a way to fit more practice into your schedule.

- If you became frustrated, determine the source of the frustration and eliminate it.

Remember, golf improvement is a process. It requires time and a good map. So, pay attention to your thoughts, emotions, and practice patterns. And, provide yourself all the time you need to cross the finish line.

Glimpses of Greatness

Even when you stay focused on one change at a time and practice diligently, the improvement process may still have its ups and downs. Some days you will feel like you're ready to take on the world, and other days you might feel like the victim of a body snatcher.

From the very beginning, though, you will see glimpses of greatness. Now and then, your "10" practice swing will show up, and you'll hit a sensational shot.

I've heard students yell with happiness and watched them tear up with joy during their very first lessons after hitting, "the best shot of their lives." I've also heard some of these same students, only one week later, question what they're doing and ask, "Why can't I get this?" expecting to see their "best shots ever" every time they hit the ball.

It's likely you will hit many more bad shots than good ones early on. But, rather than think you're "not getting it," look at your occasional great shots as signs of things to come and as confirmation that you're moving in the right direction.

How to Beat the Biggest Challenge

By far, the biggest challenge for most golfers is sticking with one step until completion.

The continual stream of swing tips and unsolicited advice, combined with the unrealistic expectation of how long it takes to make a change, form a powerful force against permanent change.

Don't be led astray! Here are some suggestions to help you stay on track:

- Write down the specific step you choose each month
- Post each step where you will see it often (i.e., on your desk, in your car, or on the bathroom mirror)
- Stick with one change per month
- Focus on multiple steps only when you are successful at completing one step per month
- Schedule your practice ahead of time like you would for any important business meeting
- Find a practice buddy so you can help each other
- Work with an I-Swing System Certified Professional
- Choose a fitting reward for each step
- Enlist the help of a friend or family member to provide rewards and keep you on track
- Use a practice journal

We all go through cycles. Consequently, our practice sessions will cycle as well. The key is to stick with it. Don't let the low times derail you. Stay on track, "Rehearse-Rate-Repeat," and keep going until you cross the finish line.

Over time, as your awareness increases, you will see more and more glimpses of greatness.

Be Your Own Best Coach

To ensure the improvement process moves forward as smoothly as possible, it pays to learn how to coach yourself.

Make sure you understand the four aspects of impact so you know what causes your shots to go where they go and do what they do. Trust yourself to find the swing that fits your body best.

Don't rely on what someone tells you about your swing. Make the commitment to feel what you're doing for yourself.

Learn everything you can about your mind, your body, your golf equipment, and anything else that has to do with your golf game. Celebrate your strengths and continue to improve in the areas needing improvement.

Your golf game is ultimately your responsibility ... and that's a good thing! You know yourself better than anyone else, and you spend more time with yourself than anyone else does. Therefore, you are usually in the best position to help yourself.

That certainly doesn't mean you need to go it alone all the time. Part of being your own best coach is seeking help when you need it. So, get your questions answered, hire a coach when you need one, and do whatever it takes to achieve your goals.

Celebrate the Good Things

One of the best ways you can help yourself is to get EXCITED about everything good you do.

Emotion is like glue. It helps anchor experiences in your brain. The more you want something to stick in your brain, the more emotional you want to get about it.

If you act like a cool cucumber when you do something well (i.e., emotionless and blasé), and you get emotional when you make a mistake (i.e., angry or frustrated), guess which makes a more memorable impression on your brain?

Any time you do something positive, GET EXCITED! Say "YES!", pump your fist, raise your hands overhead, jump up and down, or smile inside. Do something that tells your brain, "YES! That's what I want!"

I-Swing System Certified Professionals Help You Coach Yourself

You've probably heard the famous Chinese Proverb:

> *"Give a man a fish and you feed him for a day.
> Teach a man to fish and you feed him for a
> lifetime."*

I-Swing System Certified Professionals have a similar belief:

> *"Give a golfer a swing tip and it may last for a day.
> Teach a golfer to coach himself and his swing will
> improve for a lifetime."*

The Future of Golf Instruction

Traditionally, golf lessons are 30 to 60 minutes long and taken once a week on average. Often, something new is covered in every lesson.

For example, you may focus on setup in one lesson, backswing in another, and forward swing in another. Next, you may follow those three full swing lessons with a putting lesson, chipping lesson, pitching lesson, and sand lesson.

For new golfers, this "overview" approach may provide a good introduction. But, for an experienced golfer wanting permanent change, this approach is far from ideal.

I'm a strong believer in keeping practice sessions fresh and fun, but beginning something new before finishing what you've started often has negative consequences.

Here's my recommendation. Take one lesson to choose your most important step and learn the feel of exactly what you want. Then, take follow-up lessons on that same change until it's complete. This formula will keep you on track.

In the future, instead of buying a series of lessons that introduce something new every week, I foresee golfers buying a series of "changes." Each change will include an initial goal-setting session (to clarify the step you plan to take), and follow-up/supervised practice sessions designed to keep you on track until the change is complete.

Every time you complete a step, you and your coach will CELEBRATE with some kind of official graduation ceremony. Then, when you're ready to continue, you will move on to the next "change" in your series.

That's the recipe for continued improvement – one successful step at a time!

10 Ways an I-Swing System Certified Professional Can Help You

He or she can help you:

1. Solidify your image of the swing you want

2. See what you can't see until you can gather the feedback for yourself

3. Choose the most important change you need to make

4. Understand what you need to change at impact to get the results you want

5. Learn how to follow the "Ideal Practice R-R-Routine" more effectively

6. Optimize your current swing habit

7. Find the swing that feels best to your body

8. Develop the confidence to trust your own intuition

9. Answer any questions you may have

10. Stay on track until you cross the finish line

www.NexStepGolf.com

Continued Success!

"Golf is a game that can never be mastered." Early on, I took that sage advice to mean that I would be working on my golf swing for as long as I played the game.

As I worked year after year, searching for a swing that would satisfy me, the idea that I would be working on my swing *forever* was proving to be true.

Then, after more than 15 years, I finally found it. It turns out that my swing was very easy to find once I knew where to look.

And, it didn't take a lifetime.

While it may be true that the game of golf can never be mastered, it's the mental, emotional, and spiritual aspects that hold the lifelong challenge, not the swing itself.

It is absolutely possible to reach a time when you are truly satisfied with the mechanics of your golf swing.

You can develop a swing that creates the maximum power for your body and consistently produces the results you want.

And, best of all, you can own a swing that feels great – a smooth, effortless motion perfectly suited for the unique characteristics of your body.

All this can be yours – and relatively quickly and easily – when you Custom-Fit YOUR Golf Swing!

So, let's raise a glass and toast to your future. May this book inspire you to take every step to the finish line, and may you enjoy continued success for as long as you play the game!

Have FUN on your journey, and please let me know how I can help you along the way.

Here's to You!

The
19th Hole

For Book Owners Only

www.NexStepGolf.com/clubhouse

Welcome to the Club!

This book is only the beginning. To ensure your continued success, we've included several additional tools, materials, and resources in our ONLINE CLUBHOUSE - a website area created specially for "Custom-Fit YOUR Golf Swing" owners.

FREE Unlimited Access 24/7

As the I-Swing System™ continues to grow worldwide, the ONLINE CLUBHOUSE will also serve as our meeting area. We'll answer your questions, post the latest advancements, and continually upgrade the website based on your requests. Here are just a few of the bonuses you'll receive:

- Audio Programs
- Articles and E-books
- FAQ's and "Ask a Coach"
- Extensive Training Materials
- Special Event Invitations
- Game Analysis Tools
- News and Updates
- And much more!

Meet You at the Clubhouse!

As a book owner, you can receive our exceptional collection of online training materials, upcoming events schedule, ongoing support, and much more – yours FREE at:

www.NexStepGolf.com/clubhouse

Need a Speaker?

Corporate Outings – Annual Conventions
Sales Meetings – Golf Tournaments
VIP Functions – Special Events

We offer a wide variety of inspiring and entertaining CUSTOM-FIT swing programs – options include indoor, outdoor, half-day, and full-day programs, from keynote talks to tournament clinics – for large and small groups.

Each of our DYNAMIC and MEMORABLE presentations are guaranteed to change the way you and the other members of your group approach golf improvement FOREVER!

Contact NexStep Golf Headquarters for more information:

(800) 743-4-FUN (386)

Need $$$ for a Good Cause?

Associations – Clubs – Service Groups
Charitable Organizations – Churches
Schools – Medical Research

We love using our industry-leading products and services to raise money for good causes. If you know of a cause that could use our support, please contact us. We have several exciting programs in place and are also open to new ideas.

www.NexStepGolf.com/foryourcause

For a complete list of I-Swing System™
Products and Services

www.NexStepGolf.com